TIME
Secret Societies

Band of brothers *An emblem of the Knights Templar shows two riders mounted on one horse, a symbol of the crusading warrior-monks' vow of personal poverty*

TIME

MANAGING EDITOR Richard Stengel
ART DIRECTOR D.W. Pine

Secret Societies

EDITOR Kelly Knauer
DESIGNER Ellen Fanning
PICTURE EDITOR Hillary Raskin
RESEARCH Tresa McBee
COPY EDITOR Bruce Christopher Carr

TIME INC. HOME ENTERTAINMENT

PUBLISHER Richard Fraiman
GENERAL MANAGER Steven Sandonato
EXECUTIVE DIRECTOR, MARKETING SERVICES Carol Pittard
DIRECTOR, RETAIL AND SPECIAL SALES Tom Mifsud
DIRECTOR, NEW PRODUCT DEVELOPMENT Peter Harper
ASSISTANT DIRECTOR, BOOKAZINE MARKETING Laura Adam
ASSISTANT PUBLISHING DIRECTOR, BRAND MARKETING Joy Butts
ASSOCIATE COUNSEL Helen Wan
BOOK PRODUCTION MANAGER Suzanne Janso
DESIGN AND PREPRESS MANAGER Anne-Michelle Gallero
ASSOCIATE BRAND MANAGER Michela Wilde
ASSISTANT PREPRESS MANAGER Alex Voznesenskiy

SPECIAL THANKS TO

Christine Austin, Jenny Biloon, Glenn Buonocore, Jim Childs, Susan Chodakiewicz, Rose Cirrincione, Jacqueline Fitzgerald, Carrie Frazier, Lauren Hall, Jennifer Jacobs, Brynn Joyce, Mona Li, Robert Marasco, Amy Migliaccio, Brooke Reger, Dave Rozzelle, Ilene Schreider, Adriana Tierno, Sydney Webber, Jonathan White

CONTRIBUTING WRITERS

This book includes the work of the following TIME writers: Jordan Bonfante, Wendy Cole, Richard Corliss, Bruce Crumley, Jumana Farouky, Jaime A. FlorCruz, Nancy Gibbs, Elizabeth Gleick, Paul Gray, Steven Gray, Lev Grossman, Robert Hughes, Hilary Hylton, Jeff Israely, Richard Lacayo, Terry McCarthy, Lisa McLaughlin, John Nadler, Richard N. Ostling, Andrew Purvis, Andrea Sachs, James Poniewozik, Austin Ramsey, M.J. Stephey, Cathy Booth Thomas, Mia Turner, David Van Biema, James Willwerth, Richard Woodbury

We welcome your comments and suggestions about TIME Books. Please write to us at:
TIME Books, Attention: Book Editors, P.O. Box 11016, Des Moines, IA 50336-1016

To order any of our hardcover Collector's Edition books, please call us at 1-800-327-6388.
Hours: Monday through Friday, 7 a.m.–8 p.m., or Saturday, 7 a.m.–6 p.m., Central Time.

ISBN 10: 1-60320-134-3
ISBN 13: 978-1-60320-134-6
Library of Congress Control Number: 2009940849

To enjoy TIME's real-time coverage of the news, visit: **time.com**

Guardian *This serene sphinx is not located in Egypt; it is one of two that flank the stairway of the House of the Temple, a major Masonic center in Washington that is only blocks from the U.S. Capitol*

Contents

vi Introduction: Eternal Geometries
Fictions, facts and the allure of secret societies

2 Secret Societies of the Past

4 The Lost Crusade
The decline and fall of the Knights Templar

12 Masons' Mark
Freemasons are the archetypal secret society

24 The Rosicrucians
How a fictional seer shaped the Enlightenment

26 The Illuminati
A German professor sought to change the world

28 Frauds and Forgeries
From the Priory of Sion to the Elders of Zion

30 Fraternal Societies
Skull and Bones, meet the Bohemian Grove

34 The World of Dan Brown

36 Portfolio
*A wide-ranging photo gallery explores the
rich settings of the Robert Langdon novels*

54 The Face of the Modern Thriller
Dan Brown's pursuit of the elusive best seller

60 Creeds in Hiding

62 The Gospel Truth?
Scholars give Mary Magdalene a makeover

64 The Secrets of Opus Dei
The lash, the cash —and beyond the rumors

68 The Exiles of Falun Gong
China cracks down on a spiritual group

70 Sins of the Fathers
A maverick Mormon sect battles the law

74 Adventures in the Occult
The wicked ways of Aleister Crowley

76 The Cult Mentality

78 Manson Family Values
A cult for a countercultural era

82 Led to the Slaughter
A false prophet preaches mass suicide

86 Apocalypse Now
The Branch Davidians' final stand

88 The Chosen Few
From Heaven's Gate to mass weddings

90 Outside the Law

92 When Hatred Wears a Hood
The bloody trail of the Ku Klux Klan

98 Conflicts of Blood and Oath
The twisted moral code of the Mafiosi

104 Showing the Colors
The criminal élite, on the street

Hoodwinked? *On some nights, the
Washington Monument, steeped in
Masonic imagery, can resemble a
wizard's hat—or a Ku Klux Klan hood*

Eternal Geometries

Pyramids and obelisks. The compass and square. Mystical mathematics, ancient codices and Gnostic gospels. Freemasons, the Illuminati and the All-Seeing Eye. The architecture of ascent and the recurring geometries of sacred spaces. Millions of people have enjoyed close encounters with the world of arcane symbols, offbeat philosophies and secret societies in recent years, thanks to the popular novels of Dan Brown, whose ground-breaking Harvard University symbol sleuth Robert Langdon is an expert in the study of mankind's enduring cultural signposts.

In this volume, TIME explores these mysterious realms and images, separating fact from fable and romance from reality—for it's a rare reader who puts down a Brown novel without wondering exactly which aspects of his tale are fictional and which are real. This volume reports the true stories behind such notoriously tight-lipped groups as the Mafia and the Freemasons. It probes secretive religious sects, including Opus Dei and the Fundamentalist Church of Jesus Christ of Latter Day Saints. It updates history, offering new eyewitness interviews with those who encountered such false prophets as Jim Jones and Charles Manson. It presents new perspectives on Mary Magdalene, the Knights Templar and the Ku Klux Klan. And it offers a grand tour of the enduring touchstones of Western art, religion, history, science and culture. *Secret Societies* may not match Brown's page-turners as a thrill ride, but it does boast one advantage over them: it offers just the facts, Ma'am.

Echoes *Certain geometric and symbolic forms occur over and over again in architecture and culture, in places both familiar and unexpected. A key to the images shown at right is on page 106*

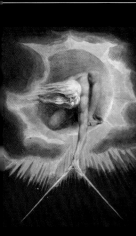
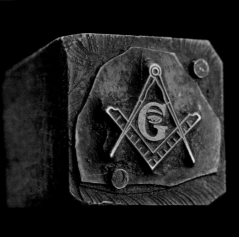

Secret Societies
of the Past

Shady proceedings
Members of California's exclusive Bohemian Grove community gather under towering redwoods north of San Francisco in 1924

The Lost Crusade

Hailed as heroic warrior-monks, the Knights Templar ended up branded as heretics and burned at the stake

Like a flaming arrow hurtling into an enemy stronghold, the Knights Templar traced a bright trajectory across the medieval sky. But if they soared to early renown and glory, the Templars came to earth abruptly in an explosive outburst of popular hysteria, accusations of Satanism, mass arrests and fiery executions. Because the two sides of the Templar coin—triumph and tragedy—were played out against the rich backdrop of the Crusades and the self-glorifying pageantry of chivalry, and because their story touches upon sacred sites and hallowed relics, this militant Christian society continues to inspire wonder and conjecture. The Templars maintain their grip on the public imagination, from Hollywood blockbusters to fast-paced best sellers.

The appeal of the Templars' story can be distilled into five words: vocation, location, organization, denunciation, immolation. As soldier-monks, these holy warriors were granted a papal dispensation that allowed them to grow into a wealthy organization that crossed national boundaries. Their headquarters on Temple Mount in Jerusalem, perhaps the single most sacred site on the planet and the location of King Solomon's celebrated Temples, intrigues those, like the Freemasons, who study the knowledge of the ancients. The financial innovations they created to organize and administer their transnational empire, which stretched at its zenith from the Holy Land across the Mediterranean and throughout Europe, made them a medieval equivalent of today's multinational corporations. And their swift downfall, amid confessions to outrageous blasphemies, was followed by the public burning of the order's leaders, ensuring their story would live in infamy.

If the Templars' chronicle ends in tragedy, it begins in piety, sacrifice and the blessing of a saint. The order was formed in the wake of one of the great turning points of history, the First Crusade, launched in 1095. In this complex clash of civilizations, Christian Europeans animated by religious fervor and the appeals of charismatic preachers staged a massive, multiyear effort to repel the growing power of Islam. The Crusade began with the appeal of the Byzantine Empire for help in its battle against militant Seljuk Turks, who were threatening to overwhelm Constantinople. Yet the Crusade quickly developed a secondary goal whose appeal came to outweigh the first: to win

A mission shared
The symbol of the Knights Templar, shown above in an engraving from circa A.D. 1150, shows two knights sharing a single horse, an emblem of the poverty of the early order

MINUT   OF THE TRIAL PUBLISHED BY

COMMIS   NERS CARDINALS BÉRENGE

ETIENN   E SUISY AND LANDOLFO

    TAINING THE TESTIMONI

back control of the sacred Christian sites in the Holy Land, especially the city of Jerusalem, from the hands of Muslims, who had controlled it for more than four centuries.

The First Crusade succeeded. Following four years of restless exertion and maneuvering, it ended in an unlikely victory for the Europeans: on July 15, 1099, a multinational army of 12,000 foot soldiers, led by some 1,200 knights on horseback, succeeded in breaching the fortresses surrounding the city of Jerusalem. Sadly, the triumphant Christian warriors disgraced themselves by slaughtering the innocent residents of the city, a blemish that has forever tarnished their victory.

The Europeans established the Kingdom of Jerusalem as the centerpiece of their foothold in the Muslim Middle East, while three smaller kingdoms formed a beachhead on the Mediterranean and a corridor into Jerusalem for pilgrims. But like any occupying army, the Christians soon found themselves and the pilgrims who followed them to the Holy Land under constant attack from angry locals, preying brigands and, eventually, major armies dedicated to overthrowing their rule. In 1119, some 300 pilgrims were murdered and 60 taken prisoner as they traveled near the River Jordan.

Enter the Knights Templar, a group of nine knights who united under the leadership of Hugh of Payens, a French knight and nobleman from the Champagne region. Distressed by the plight of the pilgrims, they proposed to the new ruler of the Kingdom of Jerusalem, Baldwin II, that they form a band of soldiers who would dedicate themselves to protecting the kingdom and its European visitors. Moreover, the knights proposed to live under holy orders, hewing to the Rule of St. Augustine. Here was a radically new notion in medi-eval religious orders: the hybrid nature of this group of would-be warrior-monks appealed to Baldwin, and he accepted their request, granting them the right to live on Temple Mount. The founding of the Knights Templar is often dated to 1118 or 1119, but the group may have been in existence several years earlier.

The new order took its name from its location: the Poor Knights of the Temple of Solomon were soon commonly called by a shorter name, the Knights Templar. Its members were housed in a captured Islamic shrine, the al-Aqsa Mosque, that remains one of the holiest sites of Islam, for Muslims believe Temple Mount is the site where the Prophet Muhammad ascended to heaven.

Like the members of all Catholic religious orders, the Templars took vows of poverty, chastity and obedience. Because they donated their worldly possessions to the order upon taking their vows, the group grew wealthy as it attracted more members. The Templars were not the only such group to be formed during the Crusades; the Knights Hospitallers devoted themselves to caring for pilgrims but were not warriors, while the Teutonic Knights were a German order of militant monks modeled after the Templars.

The Templars enjoyed the support of two powerful allies. The first was the French nobleman Hugh of Champagne, a count who renounced his worldly life to join the order; his support enhanced the Templars' reputation and enriched their coffers. (He may have been among the founders of the order; the historical record is obscure.) The second ally proved even more valuable: the charismatic monk Bernard of Clairvaux was the most respected voice in Christendom. The French

Templar Times Their rise, their fame and their downfall—in two short centuries

1095

Responding to the explosive spread of Islam in the Middle East, European Christians united in the First Crusade, left, to repel the Seljuk Turk threat to the Byzantine Empire, and also to wrest control of the sacred sites of the Holy Land from the Muslims. In July of A.D. 1099, the Crusaders took Jerusalem. With the founding of the Kingdom of Jerusalem by Christians, pilgrims from Europe began streaming into the Middle East.

1118

The Knights Templar were founded around 1118 by a group of nine French knights, led by Hugh of Payens, who sought to protect European pilgrims from brigands in the Holy Land. The

Templars found favor with King Baldwin II of Jerusalem—and with the inspirational monk Bernard of Clairvaux, who codified the order's rules. Pope Honorius II officially recognized the new order of warrior-monks at the Council of Troyes in 1128, left.

Cistercian abbot was deeply impressed with the piety and commitment of the Templars. He championed the order at a major Church meeting, the Council of Troyes, in 1128. At the council, Pope Honorius II gave the order his blessing, and Bernard codified its 73 rules in the Latin Rule. The order was directed by a Grand Master, and Hugh of Payens became the first of 23 men to hold the position.

Now blessed by both the Pope and Bernard of Clairvaux (who would be named a saint not long after his death in 1153), the Templars began to flourish. Both their ranks and their treasury swelled. Throughout Europe, admirers of what Bernard called "A New Knighthood" donated funds to the order, convinced their charity would bring them divine favor. As a result, active orders of Templars took root in England, France, Hungary, Portugal and Scotland.

In 1139, three years after Hugh of Payens' death, the Templars ascended to a higher rank within the church: Pope Innocent II elevated the order to a position of special papal

Triumph *In perhaps their most significant military victory, the Templars led the European rout of Saladin's armies at the Battle of Montgisard in 1177. Jerusalem's Temple Mount is shown in the background*

1187
The European conquest of Jerusalem in 1099 began a clash of cultures that would consume the Middle East for centuries. The Muslims found a warrior leader in Saladin, but the Europeans, led by the Templars, defeated him in 1177 at the Battle of Montgisard. In 1187 Saladin won the Battle of Hattin, right, near the Sea of Galilee, and took control of Jerusalem.

1314
Amid a series of failed Crusades in the 13th century, the Templars were gradually driven from their fortresses in the Middle East. But their power and wealth brought them enemies in Europe. In 1307 King Philip IV of France ordered a mass arrest of Templars and tortured their leaders into false confessions of blasphemy. In 1314, Grand Master Jacques de Molay was burned at the stake.

2007
After seven centuries, the Vatican released the Parchment of Chinon, which records the Templars' trials and appears to absolve them of many of their alleged transgressions.

Founding father
The first Grand Master of the Templars was French knight Hugh of Payens, shown here in an idealized 19th century portrait by Henri Charles Lehmann

privilege, granting the Templars exemption from local taxes. Later they were given the right to build their own churches. Beginning in 1147, the Templars wore a distinctive symbol, a red cross with its ends splayed against a white background.

By the mid–12th century, only 30 years after their formation, the Templars had become one of the most powerful forces in Christendom: as tax-exempt donations poured in, the order thrived. The Templars held vast tracts of land across Europe and controlled fortresses in Middle Eastern cities including Gaza, Acre, Tyre, Sidon, Beirut, Tripoli and Antioch. The organization and management of this vast empire led the Templars to become pioneers of international banking: a pilgrim could deposit funds at a Templar site in his home country, then travel across Europe and into the Middle East, drawing funds from his account. The Templars now managed a vast financial entity with locations across Europe, untaxed by local authorities and answerable only to the Vatican—another power that transcended national and regional boundaries. In short, the Templars of 1150 resembled

a modern international conglomerate. It was a formula for great success—but also for resentment and, eventually, revenge

Revenge was also on the minds of the Muslims of the Middle East, whose homelands were now occupied by European infidels. Throughout the 12th century, Muslims and Christians battled across the Holy Land, and over time, the Muslims developed warriors capable of vanquishing the Christians. The greatest of these was Salah al-Din Yusuf ibn Ayyub, known to the Western world as Saladin. This gifted and shrewd Kurdish Sunni warrior became the Sultan of Egypt, then set about driving the Christians from the Middle East.

Saladin's quest required decades of constant military activity, but it was ultimately successful. In 1177, his armies were handed a major defeat at the Battle of Montgisard outside Ramla; the Christian forces were led by the Templars, and this battle stands as their greatest military victory. But it was only a momentary setback for Saladin, who gradually won back fortress after fortress and city after city from the Christians. He handed the Templars a demoralizing defeat in 1179 at a massive fortress they were building at Jacob's Ford on the Jordan River.

In a few years Saladin won his greatest prize: his forces conquered most of the Kingdom of Jerusalem and laid siege to the holy city. On Oct. 2, 1187, Saladin's armies took control of Jerusalem, 88 years after its capture in the First Crusade. In stark contrast to the slaughter that accompanied that Christian victory, Saladin presided over a peaceful transfer of power, winning the enduring respect of his Christian foes.

Saladin's victories not only tipped the balance of power in the Holy Land; they also signaled the first step in the decline of the Templars. A Third Crusade, led by King Richard I (the Lionheart) of England, came close to capturing Jerusalem but failed. A series of later, increasingly futile, Crusades exhausted the treasuries of Europe and dampened the spiritual ardor that once had animated the cause. As the foremost exponents of the crusading spirit, the Templars saw their reputation fade as well. In 1207, Pope Innocent III issued a bull, *On Templar*

Haunts of the Templars
Befitting the Templars' hybrid role as soldiers and monks, the Knights' holdings included both churches and fortresses. Here are a few of the ancient strongholds of the Templars, where their influence can still be experienced today

Temple Church, London
Modeled after Jerusalem's Church of the Holy Sepulchre, this was the Templars' headquarters in England. The round nave at the rear of the structure dates from 1185, while the chancel at right dates to 1240.

Temple Mount, Jerusalem
This site, sacred to three religions, is where King Solomon's Temples stood and gave the order its name. The Templars' first headquarters were in al-Aqsa Mosque, one of Islam's most sacred sites. At the base of the mount is the remaining Western Wall of the Temple, where observant Jews still pray.

Kolossi Castle, Limassol, Cyprus
After Muslims regained control of Jerusalem, Europeans were gradually driven into a series of strongholds, including this fortress, built circa 1210 by the Knights Hospitallers. The lower walls at above left date to that time, but the tower was built in 1454. The Templars helped defend the fortress until their downfall early in the 14th century.

Convento de Cristo, Tomar, Portugal
The Templar church at right was built circa 1160 as part of the European campaign to resist the advances of the Moors across the Iberian peninsula.

de deux ans leur rendy leurs terrales z tout
quanque il auoit saisi du leur. Cy fine
le second liure du noble Roy philipe dieudomme.

Cy comente le tiers liure du Roy phe dieudomme
de lheresie des amories qui fu estaintez pugine.
n icellui temps flourissort a
paris philosophie z toute
clergie z y estort lestude des
sept ars surtant z ensiignt
auttorite que on ne treuue
pas quil feust onques si

Pride, that accused the order of abusing its special position within the church.

Throughout the 13th century, the Templars fought a holding action to protect their footholds in the Middle East and their reputation in Europe. Eventually, their once vast empire along the Mediterranean coast was reduced to a single fortress in Acre (in today's Israel), but in 1291 the stronghold was overrun by a powerful new set of foes from Asia Minor, the Mamluks. On the night of May 25, Templar commander Theobald Gaudin fled the fortress in a boat laden with treasure; his flight is the starting point of Raymond Khoury's popular 2007 thriller *The Last Templar.*

The Templars still clung to their fortress on the island of Cyprus, but in restless Europe, they found themselves under attack from a new foe. In France, the European stronghold of Templar power, they were now regarded with scorn and envy by the ruthless King Philip IV: he and his predecessors had often turned to the Templar treasury for loans to buttress their reign. Philip's campaign against the Templars began with his management of the selection of his handpicked French favorite, Bertrand de Got, as Pope Clement V in 1305—a victory that ushered in a long period of French domination of the papacy.

Now allied with the Pope, Philip moved against the Templars with brutal dispatch: on Oct. 13, 1307, at his order, some 5,000 French Templars were arrested, including Grand Master Jacques de Molay. Soon Christendom was rocked by sensational allegations: the Templars, ostensibly servants of Christ, were guilty of blasphemy and sacrilege: their secret initiation rites included trampling and spitting on the cross and defying the divinity of Christ. In the atmosphere of frenzy, it was even charged that the Templars worshiped a false god, a devil's head called Baphomet. Under severe torture, De Molay and other Templars confessed to such crimes. But once freed, they recanted their confessions, and most historians are confident that the Templars were innocent, a thesis reinforced after scholar Barbara Frale found a document known as the Parchment of Chinon in 2001 in the Vatican Secret Archives, where it had

been misfiled. The document indicates that Pope Clement V secretly absolved the Templars of the false charges against them, but was forced by Philip and popular frenzy to disband the order in 1312 and allow De Molay and fellow Templar Geoffrey de Charney to be burned at the stake in Paris in 1314.

Yet no Pope or King could banish the Templars from history. Their glorious heyday and incendiary downfall live on in epic novels, Hollywood blockbusters and mystical musings. Sir Walter Scott, the pioneer of the historical novel, brought the Templars to life in his highly popular novels *Ivanhoe* and *The Talisman.* Freemasons have always felt a special bond with the Templars, for the Masons trace their origins to the builders of Solomon's Temple.

In recent decades the Templars have appeared with increasing regularity in pop culture. It is an aging Templar who stands guard over the Holy Grail in Steven Spielberg's 1989 film *Indiana Jones and the Last Crusade.* Templars play a role in Dan Brown's Robert Langdon novels, especially in *The Da Vinci Code,* where they are credited with bearing and concealing the secrets of the Grail. Director Ridley Scott's 2005 film *Kingdom of Heaven* depicts the Templars as bloodthirsty opponents of Saladin. And Khoury's *The Last Templar* put the ancient warrior-monks atop the best-seller lists and in a made-for-TV miniseries. Authors Christopher Knight and Robert Lomas advanced a fascinating thesis that the image on the famed Shroud of Turin is not that of Christ, but in fact records the torture of Jacques de Molay.

But if the Templars conjure up romance in Europe and America, their legacy is taken more seriously by the contemporary jihadists of Islamic extremism. Al-Qaeda chief Osama bin Laden has declared, "Our goal is for our nation to unite in the face of the Christian crusade." In some minds, the deeds of the Knights Templar continue to sound the trumpets of battle. ■

Blasphemy? *Above, Templars are shown mocking the crucified Christ in their initiation ritual, one of the slanders brought against them.*

On facing page, the burning of De Molay and De Charney is depicted in an illuminated manuscript from the 15th century

Masons' Mark

How history's master builders, the Freemasons, lost their mojo—and how pop culture brought it back

Search *Encyclopaedia Britannica* for the word *Freemasons* and an unusual though not entirely unexpected result pops up: the entry for *scapegoats*. The highly secretive organization that once counted George Washington, Benjamin Franklin and Wolfgang Amadeus Mozart among its ranks has been a favorite target for conspiracy theorists since the early 18th century, when Masonic lodges first spread widely across Europe. But in recent decades in the U.S., Masonry has lost its magic. So when bestselling novelist Dan Brown took aim at the Masons' cultlike reputation in his 2009 thriller *The Lost Symbol,* he did them a favor. Though his account of the group's supposed stranglehold on the U.S. political scene was utterly fanciful, Brown's depiction of Masonry handed the society a present it hadn't enjoyed in years: the oxygen of publicity.

As is the case with Brown's other potboilers featuring Harvard "symbologist" Robert Langdon, the novel left readers wanting to know the real skinny on the famed secret society that puts its plot in motion: Who are the Masons, where did they come from, why have they so often served as scapegoats, and what role do they play on the world stage in the 21st century?

In many ways, Freemasonry is history's archetypal secret society. Here are all the trappings that characterize the form: membership is secret; private handshakes and secret words distinguish initiates from pre-

tenders; members ascend in the group via a series of ever more exclusive steps; and the lore and legend of the ancient world play a strong role in the culture of the lodge, whose rites and rituals have remained unchanged for centuries. Small wonder people are prepared to believe just about anything about this mysterious crew—except, it seems, the unvarnished truth.

Freemasons like to trace their origins to the great mathematicians, architects and engineers of the Classical and biblical world: Euclid, Archimedes and King Solomon. But if they share a sympathy of purpose with these ancient builders, there are no clear historical links between modern Masonry and these imposing figures. The origins of the Freemasons are more recent, if centuries old: they can be traced to the network of builders, architects and other craftsmen who created the soaring Gothic cathedrals of the Middle Ages.

The distinguishing characteristic of Freemasonry is the first term of the group's portmanteau title: the original freemasons were a trade guild composed of freemen, proudly distinguished from medieval serfs, who were bound by oaths of fealty to a local noble. Masons stood apart from other guilds because they traveled to their work, wherever a cathedral was rising. On the grounds of their projects, freemasons, set apart by the tool-carrying aprons they wore, would set up a lodge where they served meals, sketched their designs and prepared their stones. To these lodges no persons were ad-

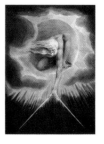

Divine measure
The English poet William Blake's painting The Ancient of Days *exemplifies the Masonic view of God as a compass-wielding Great Architect of the Universe.*

At right, a Masonic stamp, reversed for readability, includes the square and compass, the tools of medieval stonemasons, and a capital letter G, representing both God and Geometry

Heirs of Solomon

Masons like to trace their roots to the building of King Solomon's two temples in Jerusalem, as shown in the 1884 American wood engraving above.

Much Masonic lore centers on tales of legendary chief temple builder Hiram Abiff. Masons also feel a kinship with the Knights Templar, whose first home was atop Temple Mount

mitted but those initiated in the craft's mysteries, which included technical secrets of geometry and architecture, protected by sure means of identification.

Medieval masons were just as concerned with guarding their intellectual property—the mathematical know-how that transformed heavy stones into lofty cathedrals—as are today's high-tech software companies. The secrecy that has always been a hallmark of Freemasonry arose from practical necessity and caution, rather than the desire to cultivate an aura of mystery.

Some master masons kept codes of what modern managers would call "best practices"; one such 64-page chronicle from Britain, which invokes the name of Euclid, has been identified as the earliest Masonic written document to have survived. Many histo-

rians date this *Regius Poem* (also known as the Halliwell Manuscript) to A.D. 1390, but some estimates date it as late as circa 1450. It is believed to have been written by a Roman Catholic priest charged with working closely with masons on construction projects.

Analytical and productive, economically and politically independent and untethered to local nobles, freemasons composed a unique echelon in the medieval world. These minds and hands for hire stood out as sharp-eyed realists, practical men who joined the worshippers in the cathedrals they erected but also venerated the universal truths of science. Over time, their society became one of the great engines of the Age of Enlightenment, advocating for the individual rather than authority, for progress rather than tradition, for reason rather than faith.

As Europe emerged from the Middle Ages, the appeal of these ancient guilds grew: outsiders, including nobles, began to seek admission to their ranks. By 1620 there were "Accepted Masons," as well as more traditional, practicing Freemasons, in England. Bit by bit the new members predominated in the old guild, facilitating Masonry's growth and cementing its appeal to those in high places—and those eager to join them. From the beginning, Masons have been strivers and networkers, Dale Carnegies with shirt-protectors.

The transforming step that converted this ancient guild of builders into a wide-ranging society that embraced men of achievement in every field came early in the 18th century. In 1717 England's four main Masonic lodges united to form the Grand Lodge of England; within six years this powerful new central body had created a written constitution. Its writer, James Anderson, avoided the raging religious tensions of the era by stating that Masons must simply demonstrate their devotion to a Supreme Being, with no further specifications required. Anderson's term for this vague supernatural entity, "The Great Architect of the Universe," forges a perfect amalgam of religion and science: the Masonic deity is God the Architect and Builder.

Yet if Freemasonry celebrated practicality and science, it also made room for mythology and lore, ritual and flummery—much of it cloaked in secrecy. **Signs and symbols, divine architecture, Gnostic teachings, numerology and** arcane allegories: all became part of Freemasonry, if more fervently embraced by some Masons than others. Freemasons like to see themselves as belonging to a select order of merit as **old as human culture; Anderson's writings go so far as to include Moses and Noah in the ranks of Masons.**

Masons were firmly committed to egalitarianism, civic participation and other ideals, but these were expressed through tropes of the stoneworkers trade: the square for straightforward virtue; the compass to circumscribe one's passions; the plumb line to stay upright. There was little religion but much ritual, which enraged churchmen and engaged conspiracy theorists.

Milestones of the Masons

Medieval Guilds

Stonemasons at work, as shown in a stained-glass window at Chartres Cathedral, created circa 1250. The compass at top right and the two right-angle squares at bottom right are among the enduring symbols of Freemasonry.

Regius Poem

This document, also called the Halliwell Manuscript, lays out the "best practices" of medieval mason-builders and associates them with Euclid and ancient engineers. Dated to 1390-1450, its significance as a precursor of Masonry was first noted by antiquarian and Shakespeare scholar James Halliwell in 1840.

Goose and Gridiron

Modern Freemasonry took shape at this London tavern in 1717, when four British Masonic lodges agreed to combine themselves into the Grand Lodge of England. Four years later the group changed its name to Premier Grand Lodge of England; in 1723 it published the first Masonic constitution, still in force.

Paris Commune

Freemasonry was a driving wheel of the Age of Enlightenment, helping spur the American and French revolutions. In 1871, 10,000 French Freemasons marched to support the anti-authoritarian uprising of the Paris Commune.

Léo Taxil's Slanders

A French gadfly, Taxil published incendiary pamphlets in the late 1800s accusing Masons of conducting Satanic rites. In 1897 he stunned France by admitting the charges were utterly fanciful, no more than a hoax. But his slurs have continued to percolate, tarnishing Masonry's image.

As Masonry spread, different versions arose; today's Scottish Rite and York Rite groups reflect divisions that took place during the explosive growth of lodges across Europe in the 18th century. The buzz was amplified by the Freemasons' insistence on privacy: once essential to protecting the tools of the stonemasons' trade, the group's secrecy became an end in itself, fueling the exclusive status that made membership so desirable while reinforcing the belief that Masons had something to hide.

Freemasonry reached Britain's American colonies early, but the first "regular" lodge was established in Boston in 1733. Masons played key roles in the Continental Congress: the brotherhood helped unite the leaders of the squabbling colonies and primed them for that quintessential Enlightenment political enterprise, the American Revolution. Colonial lodges, says Masonic historian William Moore, offered "a civil space in which to play with self-rule in a world where democracy was not yet a fact."

Benjamin Franklin joined a Philadelphia lodge and, during his years in France, guided Voltaire through the order's mysteries. George Washington was initiated into a Scottish Rite lodge at Fredericksburg, Va., in 1752. When he was inaugurated in Manhattan as first President of the U.S., the grand master of the New York lodge administered the oath. Within decades, so many officials of the early Republic were Masons that in 1826 an Anti-Masonic Party was organized.

In Europe, Masonry harbored the free-thinking achievers who had long been restless under old regimes. In France, where the church and the throne had long maintained a tight grip over society, candidates for admission did not have to state their belief in a higher being to join a lodge. French Masons generally supported the 1789 revolution, and they played a major role in the events of 1871, when the Paris Commune presented a serious threat to the national government in the wake of the lost Franco-Prussian War. Masons marched en masse in support of the Communards, but the uprising was brutally suppressed.

European Masonry lost its revolutionary charge in the 20th century and became pre-

Reborn *In some rites, Masons can progress by stages through 33 degrees of membership, but many Masons do not progress beyond the third degree, earning the title of Master Mason. That initiation often includes a symbolic death and rebirth, representing a new state of consciousness. Below, the rite is depicted in an 18th century French drawing*

Freemasonry in the U.S.

Masons played key roles in shaping the Republic

Laying Democracy's Foundations

That Masons placed their stamp on early America has been well documented, although the group's influence has been exaggerated by the society's more booster-ish brethren and in such films as *National Treasure* (2004). George Washington was the grand master of his Virginia lodge, and he presided over the placing of the cornerstone of the U.S. Capitol building in 1793, wearing his Mason's apron, as depicted in the 1942 painting by John Melius, above. Masons also famously placed a special stone in the White House; TIME's late Washington correspondent Hugh Sidey described in an amusing 2000 article the repeated attempts over the years to locate the stone, which have employed mine-sweepers, radar and a pair of dowsers. The cornerstone has never been found, even when the building was almost completely gutted and rebuilt in the late 1940s.

Prince Hall Masons

America's Masonic lodges were as segregated as the rest of U.S. society until recent decades. But African Americans formed their own network of Prince Hall lodges, named for a Massachusetts man who is believed to have served in the Revolutionary Army. Above, members of a Prince Hall lodge in Brooklyn in 1907.

The Anti-Masonic Party

When rejected would-be Mason William Morgan threatened to publish alleged Masonic intrigues, he was arrested and later disap-peared, in 1826, above. His book was published, igniting a popular revolt against the society, which included the founding of the Anti-Masonic Party, whose influence was regional and short-lived.

Dollar Bill

The Great Seal of the U.S., approved in 1782, includes such Masonic imag-ery as an unfinished pyramid and an All-Seeing Eye. *Annuit Coeptis* means "He (God) Favors Our Undertakings." The Latin phrase for "New World Order" at the bottom was a rallying cry of the Enlightenment. The seal was placed on the dollar bill by President Franklin D. Roosevelt, a Mason.

cisely what it had once opposed: a guardian of society's status quo. In many countries membership became a potent lever for professional advancement, leading to charges that Masons constituted a powerful, sinister, behind-the-scenes force that united business interests and political parties.

If such allegations ring false to American ears, they merit more credence in Europe. A Vatican banking scandal in the early 1980s involved a Masonic lodge dominated by Italian mafiosi. In the late '90s, Britain's Parliament conducted two inquiries into allegations that Masonic corruption pervaded the nation's police forces and judiciary. In France in 1999 the public prosecutor of Nice, Eric de Montgolfier, denounced the "networks of Freemasons" that, he said, were exerting an undue influence on the region's judiciary. Months later it was revealed that Alain Bartoli, a Nice police officer and a Freemason, had used a law-enforcement database to conduct extensive background searches on several people, including De Montgolfier and then President Jacques Chirac.

Masonry's influence in the U.S., once strong, has declined over time. By 1830 its members' near monopoly on government positions—and a scandal over the mysterious disappearance of a Mason who broke secrecy—provoked the birth of U.S. single-issue politics: the Anti-Masonic Party nearly wiped the group out. The Masons eventually bounced back as the preferred club of America's merchant class— the Straus family reportedly built Masonic columns into New York City's Macy's department store—and again as political incubator. After World War II, returning G.I.s seeking to maintain the fraternity and patriotism of Army life swelled the rosters of lodges.

Over time, U.S. Masonry evolved into a more purely social organization, focusing its energy on charitable works and civic im-

Masons at the Met *In its early years, European Masonry attracted such luminaries as Mozart, whose 1791 opera* The Magic Flute *is saturated in Masonic imagery, as reflected in this 2004 production at New York City's Metropolitan Opera, directed and designed by Julie Taymor*

© KEN HOWARD/THE METROPOLITAN OPERA

provement. In a nation of joiners, Masons competed for members with such fraternal groups as the Elks and Knights of Pythias and with such interest groups as Rotary International and Chambers of Commerce. The transformation was embodied in the huge growth of the Masonic offshoot the Shriners. This highly fraternal branch of Masonry is technically titled the Ancient Arabic Order of the Nobles of the Mystic Shrine. In reality, most Shriners are neither ancient nor Arabic, noble or mystic. But they are undeniably sociable, well meaning and charitable.

A 1949 TIME cover story captured the last great heyday of U.S. Masonry, as it described the convergence of some 75,000 Masons in Chicago to celebrate the diamond jubilee of the Shriner movement in the U.S. at an annual convention. "The first big event on the schedule was the parade down Michigan Avenue: … the Medinah (Ill.) nobles in $42,500 worth of new uniforms; the country's leading citizens decked out like Zouaves and harem guards … 1,000 chanters (glee clubs), drill teams …" And so on.

Freemasonry's U.S. branch reached a high point in 1959, when it constituted an earnest and convivial army of 4.1 million. Yet as of 2010 its ranks have been depleted by more than 60%: in 2008, the last year for which figures are available, the national membership of Master Masons numbered 1.44 million. Even so, the group remains a major philanthropic presence, donating some $750 million a year to charities.

Yet if Freemasonry's influence in the real world has declined precipitately in recent decades, it has flourished in the alternate reality of pop-culture mythology. The society's secrecy, its ancient antecedents, its ritual trappings: all exert a magnetic spell on the creators of thriller novels and Hollywood epics. Like the Knights Templar, Masons open a portal to a world rich in pageantry, ritual and mystery. The organization was catapulted into the pop-culture firmament by thriller writer Brown, whose three Robert Langdon novels restore the mystery to Masonry. Though Masons play a role in both *Angels & Demons* and *The Da*

A Masonic All-Star Team
Modern Masons who left a mark

JOSEPH SMITH
The founding prophet of the Church of Jesus Christ of Latter-Day Saints wove elements of Masonic lore into Mormonism. One of his multiple wives was the widow of William Morgan, whose allegations led to the founding of the Anti-Masonic Party.

MARK TWAIN
Samuel Clemens joined a St. Louis lodge in 1861 but was not an active Mason for long. In *Huckleberry Finn,* young Huck proclaims himself "Royal Grand Warden to the Knights of Morality, and Sublime Grand Marshal of the Good Templars."

WILLIAM HOWARD TAFT
The 27th President was initiated into a Cincinnati lodge "at sight" in 1909 and attended a special session at a Philadelphia lodge in 1912. After his single term in office, he served as Chief Justice of the U.S.

HENRY FORD
The man whose affordable cars changed American life was a member of Palestine Lodge No. 357 in Detroit. His famed remark, "History is more or less bunk. We don't want tradition," seems at odds with Masonry's emphasis on celebrating heritage.

Vinci Code, they take center stage in the 2009 best seller *The Lost Symbol,* where they are depicted as a highly potent force in Washington, D.C.

Surprisingly, novelist Brown found himself scooped on his own turf by the 2004 film *National Treasure,* which applied the Langdon formula to U.S. history five years before Brown published *The Lost Symbol.* As for the accuracy of that book's depiction of Masonic influence: much as TIME would like to report that Masons do indeed exert surprising sway over the American political landscape, it is our duty to state that the objects one sees in Brown's fictional magic mirror often appear larger than they are in reality.

To learn more about today's Masons, TIME interviewed author Jay Kinney, whose book *The Masonic Myth* attempts to dispel some of the persistent rumors about the group. Here's how Kinney described his own

Separate—but equal? *Worldwide Masonry's longtime exclusion of female members, still widely in force today, marched in lock step with society's relegation of women to secondary roles. Eventually, women were welcomed by some lodges; the Order of the Eastern Star is the most well known. Members of a British women's lodge are shown above in 1937*

HARRY HOUDINI
Born in Hungary as Ehrich Weisz, the magician joined a New York City lodge in 1923 and gave performances to raise funds for Masonic charities. He was a foe of fraudulent spiritualists, whose fakery he loved to expose.

WINSTON CHURCHILL
The British statesman's father Randolph was a Mason. Churchill, a joiner by nature, was initiated into a London lodge in 1901, at the beginning of his political career, but had little time to devote to Masonic affairs.

J. EDGAR HOOVER
The longtime head of the FBI is one of the greatest keepers of secrets in U.S. history. He became a third-degree Mason, or Master Mason, in a Washington, D.C., lodge in 1920.

THURGOOD MARSHALL
The first African American to serve on the U.S. Supreme Court won the historic 1954 decision that desegregated America's schools. He was a member of a Prince Hall lodge, the African-American branch of U.S. Masonry.

TOPICAL PRESS AGENCY/GETTY IMAGES

21

initiation rite: "When I showed up, I was put in a little preparation room beforehand that had some clothing that I was supposed to put on, and then they gave me a blindfold," he told TIME. "The 'obligation,' or oath, is done at the altar in the middle of the lodge room. It's basically just a waist-high piece of furniture that has a Bible or whatever sacred text the individual has for their particular religion. Then you're walked around the lodge room, introduced to each of the main officers. You see the assembled brethren and the master of the lodge before you in his top hat. It's very traditional, early-1800s garb. And after the ritual—and this is true of all the Masonic degrees—the master recites a lecture on the group's history and symbols, memorized word for word. Those haven't changed in 200 years."

Lest Masons accuse Kinney of betraying the group's secrets, he refused to tell all in his book. "The consensus seemed to be that the specific means Masons use to recognize each other—handshakes, the specific wording of parts of the ritual—should not be divulged. You don't want some fake Mason coming to your lodge and talking their way into your meetings," he explained. For the record, today's Freemasons insist that tattletales are no longer—if ever they were—held to their promise to "having my throat cut across, my tongue torn out … and buried in the sands of the sea," as the initiation reads in part. Some of other details of the initiation ceremony—the rolled-up pants leg, the blindfolded symbolic journey—have long been widely known.

Like many other current observers, Kinney expressed his regret that U.S. Masonry is in a period of decline, as its membership ages and the next cohort of initiates is nowhere on the horizon. When TIME asked Kinney to describe what Masons actually do, his reply encapsulated the dual goals of the modern society: "The outer mission is to be of service to the greater community, donating to charities and Masonic youth groups, like the Order of DeMolay for boys and Rainbow Girls, which encourage kids to be good citizens and give them social circles that are supervised by adults and are more positive than hanging out on street corners. The organization is also based on a kind of stoic philosophy, to become the master of your own passions—don't fall prey to your emotions, to anger—and to have a sort of balanced perspective on life."

Laying the foundations to create a better society and better individuals; if those goals may seem a tad less spectacular than erecting Chartres Cathedral or running the world from secret hideouts, it is still eminently worthy. It's good to know that, some 800 years after they first began to emerge as a force on the world stage, Masons are still in the business of building. ∎

Masonic Emblems And Symbols

Masonic imagery draws from a wide variety of sources, including the tools of medieval trade guilds, ancient and Gnostic lore and the works of legendary builders of the past. The Masonic poster at right, published in New York City in 1908, incorporates many of the most famous symbols of the society.

1. The Eye Commonly called the "All-Seeing Eye" or the "Eye of Providence," this ancient image of omniscient knowledge is a reference to the Supreme Being whose existence most Masons must acknowledge. Placed atop a pyramid, the eye appears on the Great Seal of the U.S. on the reverse side of the dollar bill. The origins of the symbol have been traced to ancient Egypt.

2. Letter G The capital letter, often placed within a compass and square in Masonic emblems, refers to God the Architect and also to geometry.

3. The Temple Masons look to the builders of Solomon's two Temples in Jerusalem as the pioneers of their craft, or knowledge.

4. The Handshake The Mason's famed secret greeting originated in the need to recognize fellow initiates in the trade secrets of medieval building.

5. Initiation This scene depicts the lectern, sacred book, square and compass that are all part of the initiation ritual of Masonic lodges.

6. The Pillars The two tall, slender obelisks—which can be crowned with globes, pyramids or orbs of light—refer to the pillars of Solomon's Temple. The obelisk was a favored monumental form of ancient Egypt. Note the twin pillars in the Metropolitan Opera production of Mozart's *The Magic Flute* shown earlier in this story.

7. The Beehive This emblem of industry and cooperation reminds Masons that they should never be idle, for their efforts can be of great benefit to their fellow man.

8. The Vignettes The scenes surrounding the central panel show a variety of images significant to Masonry. On the left side, we see Hiram Abiff imparting knowledge at the top, Noah's Ark, and the lambskin apron worn by all Masons. At the bottom center, two Masons exchange a secret handshake of fraternity. At bottom right are the tools of the craft: a compass, a square and other devices.

The vignettes on the right side include images of Justice, of the symbolic death undergone by Master Masons, and of the five noble orders of architecture, represented by five ascending pillars.

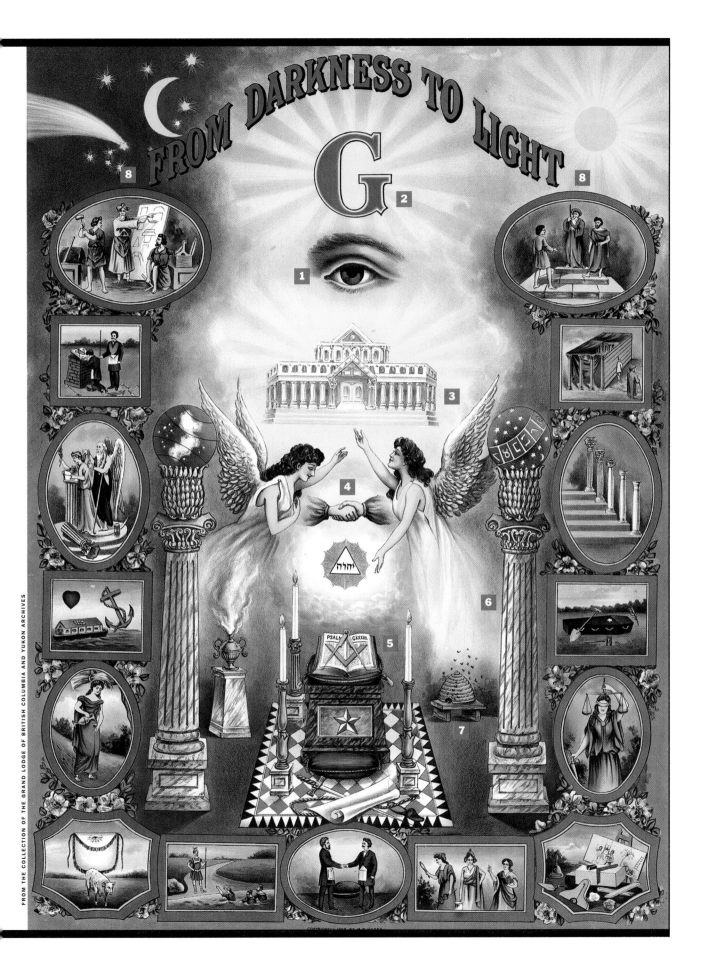

FROM DARKNESS TO LIGHT

The Rosicrucians
The mystical underpinnings of modern science

The founder of Rosicrucianism is an allegorical figure who never existed. The mythical order's founding texts were published anonymously and are the sort of elaborate literary hoaxes that contemporary critics call "metafictions." Generations of Americans are familiar with a profit-driven modern incarnation of Rosicrucianism whose cheesy, portentous ads appear in magazines and comic books and whose most prominent current presence is a tourist attraction in San Jose, Calif., the Rosicrucian Egyptian Museum and Planetarium. Sound bogus? Yet the potent force that initially powered Rosicrucianism—the attempt to rediscover ancient knowledge via close study of the natural world—helped spark the Enlightenment.

The "Order of the Rosy Cross" has its origins in the turmoil of the Protestant Reformation in Germany. The existence of this fictitious secret society of learned men was revealed in three works published anonymously in Germany, *Fama Fraternitatis Roseae Crucis* (The Fame of the Brotherhood of RC, 1614), *Confessio Fraternitatis Roseae Crucis* (The Confession of the Brotherhood of RC, 1615) and *The Chemical Wedding of Chrstian Rosenkreuz,* 1616. The works describe the life of "C.R.C.," the mythical Christian Rosenkreuz (German for "rose cross"). He is portrayed as a seeker who acquired mystical knowledge dating back to the ancient Greeks in the Middle East, then returned to Europe to found a brotherhood composed of eight philosopher/alchemist/physicians devoted to healing the sick.

These manifestos struck a nerve in a Europe riven by religious strife and still buzzing with the fascination with the Classical world that first emerged during the Renaissance. The Order of the Rosy Cross may have been vaporware, but its anti-Catholic, pro-Reformation ideology inspired those with probing minds who believed that intellectual inquiry could deliver mankind from waging war over religion and politics. In what British scholar Frances Yates called "the Rosicrucian Enlightenment," the spirit of hands-on investigation called for by this idealized group helped inspire the loose collaboration of pioneering natural scientists

that 17th century British chemist Robert Boyle called the "Invisible College."

Rosicrucianism was first presented to the world cloaked in mysticism, but its lasting impact was to lay the groundwork for modern science based on the experimental method. Yet in popular lore, this fictitious brotherhood lingers on as a sort of cultural attic, a home for spiritual fads ranging from alchemy to Gnostic mysteries to astrology. Its influence in that debased form can still be seen in the works of 20th century French Surrealist artists; TIME's veteran art critic Robert Hughes dismissed that contribution in two words: "mystical gobbledygook." ■

Battling for free thought *At right is the frontispiece from the* Collegium Fama Fraternitatis *(1618) by "Theophilus Schweighardt," a.k.a. Daniel Mogling, a response to the founding documents of Rosicrucianism. Steeped in allegorical symbols, the engraving depicts the Fraternal College of Rosicrucianism as an armored enclave of inquiry, traveling through a Europe wasted by religious and political battles.*

At left is a 1629 painting of a rose with a cruciform stem. The Latin phrase reads, "The rose gives the bees honey," merging Rosicrucianism with the beehive, a symbol of industry also used in Freemasonry

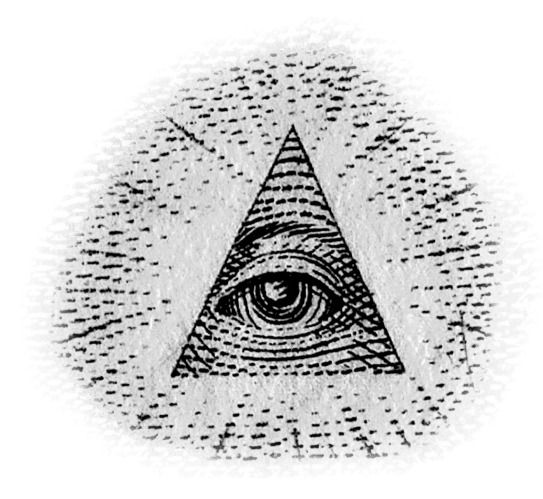

The Illuminati

A Bavarian professor sought to change the world, not rule it

Who are the Illuminati? Well, according to the website *illuminati-news.com,* this mysterious group is "... a super-rich Power Elite with an ambition to create a slave society! The Illuminati are ... the men who really rule the world from behind the scenes ... They are connected by bloodlines going back thousands and thousands of years in time ... [Their] main goal is to create a One World Government, with them on top to rule the world into slavery and dictatorship. George Bush Sr. and a few other major players ... have openly called for a New World Order ... The Elite that controls the societies and the Illuminati are occultists and black magicians. They say their God is Lucifer, 'The Light Bearer,' and by occult practices they manipulate and influence the masses ..."

And so on. But while this description certainly illuminates the mind-set of its author and summarizes some of the popular myths surrounding a branch of the European Enlightenment that has long been dormant, it fails to shed light on the Illuminati themselves. So here is an alternate history, one that is accurate if substantially less entertaining and imaginative.

Like the Rosicrucians who preceded them on the world stage, the Illuminati began as a self-selected group of intellectuals seeking to free themselves from age-old chains of church and state. The visionary of the Bavarian Order of the Illuminati was Adam Weishaupt (1748-1830), a Freemason and professor of canon law at the University of Ingolstadt in Germany. He published the founding document of the group he initially called "the Order of Perfectibilists" in 1776, a good year for laying foundations. Indeed, Weishaupt's call to action mirrored the intellectual currents that were driving the American Revolution: "… to raise liberty from its ashes—to restore to man his original rights … to obtain an eternal victory over oppressors—and to work the redemption of mankind, in secret schools of wisdom."

The words might be those of Thomas Jefferson—until Weishaupt's screed reaches a tipping point, calling for a secret society of initiates to lead the rebellion against authority, as opposed to the American leader's view of a broadly based public movement for freedom. Even so, Jefferson defended Weishaupt's scheme for his fellow radicals to infiltrate Masonic lodges, whose secrecy would protect them. In a letter to the president of The College of William and Mary), Jefferson wrote, "As Wishaupt [sic] lived under the tyranny of a despot & priests, he knew that caution was necessary even in spreading information, & the principles of pure morality. He proposed therefore to lead the Free masons to adopt this object & to make the objects of their institution the diffusion of science & virtue."

Yet Weishaupt erred in diffusing his views a bit too widely, and he was dismissed from his teaching post and exiled from Bavaria by its Elector, Karl Theodor, in 1785. He spent the remainder of his life in Gotha, a town in Thuringia, protected by sympathetic nobles, writing books explaining his views. Those free-thinking views, and the tropes in which he expressed them—including the all-seeing eye adapted from Egyptian mythology, the urge to wrest "order from chaos," and the search for an enlightened *Novus Ordo Seclorum,* or New World Order—continued to percolate through Europe and the U.S., some ultimately landing on the back of the U.S. dollar bill and, more recently, in the popular video game *Deus Ex* and in Hollywood movies.

The Illuminati, like the Rosicrucians, live on in popular culture, a handy magnet for suspicion and rumor, and for conspiracy theorists who view a Bavarian professor's failed attempt to institute a New World Order as an enterprise that still thrives in the form of a shadowy super-élite. That powerful group includes TIME magazine, according to one strident Christian website, which noted that the magazine named New York City mayor Rudolph Giuliani its Person of the Year in the wake of the 9/11 terrorist attacks. "TIME attributed him as the one man to bring order out of chaos to New York after the WTC disaster," said the site. "I honestly don't know how they can get any more blatant in their satanic symbolism." Busted! ∎

Freedom! *The painting above,* An Allegory of the Revolution with a Portrait Medallion of Jean-Jacques Rousseau, *by Nicolas Henri Jeaurat de Bertry, associates some of the symbols employed by Adam Weishaupt, right, founder of the Illuminati, with the French Revolution. The all-seeing eye, the most prominent symbol of the Illuminati, is above the French flags. A pyramid, representing man's urge to ascend, is at rear. The image is used by both Freemasons and the Illuminati*

Frauds and Forgeries

History is littered with elaborate hoaxes that supposedly expose the dark schemes of secret societies. The targets range from despised minorities to the wealthy and influential, and some of the slanders have proved deadly

C'est vrai? Non!
In *The Da Vinci Code,* a window with the letters *P* and *S* at the Church of St. Sulpice in Paris stands for the Priory of Sion. In fact, the letters honor Saints Pierre and Sulpice, the two patrons of the church.

Renaissance genius Leonardo, above, is named as a grand master of the Priory, a claim as false as the supposed secret society itself

The Priory of Sion

"Fact: the Priory of Sion—a European secret society founded in 1099—is a real organization. In 1975 Paris's Bibliothèque Nationale discovered parchments known as *Les Dossiers Secrets,* identifying numerous members of the Priory of Sion, including Sir Isaac Newton, Botticelli, Victor Hugo and Leonardo da Vinci." This note, inserted by novelist Dan Brown before the text of his novel *The Da Vinci Code* begins, has managed to hornswoggle millions of readers. So … here's a Take 2 on the subject.

"Fact: the Priory of Sion is a mythical secret society, a hoax created by French gadfly Pierre Plantard (1920-2000), who planted false documents supposedly proving the existence of the Priory in the official National Library of France." This definition, if less vivid than the first, is superior in one respect: it is accurate. The Priory, according to Plantard's documents, was set up to protect France's line of Merovingian kings, who bore a dark secret: their bloodline was descended from

the union of Jesus Christ and Mary Magdalene, a fact potentially so destructive to the authority of the Church that it was deliberately suppressed by the Vatican.

Well, it's a great tale, as the sales of *The Da Vinci Code* attest. And Brown appropriated Plantard's hoax brilliantly, using it to propel the fast-paced plot of his thriller. The creation of this fantastical organization falls into a category of alternate history and metafiction with a long provenance in Europe, stretching from Cervantes' *Don Quixote* and the allegorical founding texts of Rosicrucianism to the dazzling fictions of Umberto Eco. As for Plantard, writer Arthur Goldwag, whose book *Cults, Conspiracies & Secret Societies* (Vintage; 2009) is an informative, no-nonsense survey of this territory, describes him as "a longtime ultranationalist and anti-Semite and a convicted swindler with a prison record." Plantard eventually confessed that the documents he placed in the Bibliotheque Nationale were forgeries.

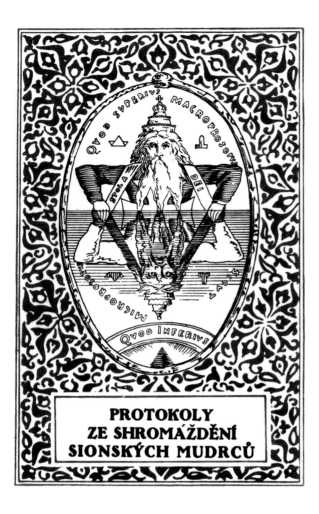

Protocols of the Elders of Zion

"I hope the time will come," Judge Walter Meyer declared in a courtroom in Berne, Switzerland, "when people everywhere will be astonished to learn that in the year 1935 it was necessary to talk for 17 days about possible authenticity in this incredible nonsense which is called *The Protocols of the Elders of Zion*." Sadly, 75 years after that libel trial, this hoax, perhaps the most successfully insidious and destructive forgery in history, continues to feed anti-Semitism around the world. Describing a conspiracy at the highest levels of Judaism to dominate the world by stealth, it first was aired in a St. Petersburg newspaper in 1903. The origins of the slur have been traced to secret police agents in Czar Nicholas II's court who hoped to discredit radical and progressive groups within Russia by making them appear dupes of alien Jewish machinations. The contents have been traced to a German novel and a French satirical essay, but no matter: the bait is swallowed wherever anti-Semitism is active. A German printing went through 33 editions before Adolf Hitler became Chancellor in 1933, and the *Protocols* are widely accepted as true in today's Middle East, where they are held up as proof of Zionist intrigue by Israel's many enemies in the region.

Trilateral Commission

If conspiracy allegations were quills, banker and philanthropist David Rockefeller would be a porcupine. Rockefeller belongs to a number of high-level international groups that are frequently accused by conspiracy buffs of plotting to take over the world. Among these supposedly sinister organizations: the Trilateral Commission, a non-governmental organization founded by Rockefeller in 1973 to advocate for improvements in international understanding and financial systems, and the Bilderberg conference, an annual multinational gathering, first held in the Netherlands, to promote international harmony.

Surprisingly, the World Economic Forum, held annually in Davos, Switzerland—which brings together movers and shakers from industry, technology and finance—still seems to be off the radar of those who enjoy imagining that the world is really operated by secret, scheming cabals of the influential. Prediction: Stay tuned.

Fraternal Societies

Across America, college students, executives, society folk and civic boosters come together in exclusive groups that share some of the outward trappings—if little of the historic underpinnings—of such better-known secret societies as the Freemasons

Skull and Bones

Conspiracy theories about American education's most notorious secret society, Yale University's Skull and Bones Society, are almost as old as the society itself. The group has been blamed for everything from the creation of the nuclear bomb to the Kennedy assassination. It's been aped in bad teen horror films and satirized—along with fellow conspiracy-group targets the Freemasons and the Illuminati—in *The Simpsons*. Its home, a satisfyingly gloomy, windowless fortress in New Haven, Conn., is called "the Tomb." Top that, Phi Beta Kappa!

Minus the trappings of wealth, privilege and power, Skull and Bones could be a laughably juvenile club for *Dungeons & Dragons* geeks. But its rumored alumni have made up a disproportionately large percentage of the world's most influential leaders. Bonesmen have, at one time, controlled the fortunes of the Carnegie, Rockefeller and Ford families, as well as posts in the Central Intelligence Agency, the American Psychological Association, the Council on Foreign Relations and some of the world's most powerful law firms.

A Yale undergrad named William Russell founded the group in 1832 after spending a year in Germany among members of some of the most mystical and élite clubs in the world, including organizations that mimicked the Enlightenment-era Illuminati. Russell returned to the U.S. determined to found a secret society of his own and "tapped" Alphonso Taft, whose son would later become President William H. Taft, to be among the first members of "The Brotherhood of Death," or, as it was initially more formally known, "The Order of the Skull and Bones."

The group picks its members in a highly confidential manner. Yale juniors are tapped for membership each

Geronimo

spring, receiving an envelope sealed with a black wax stamp bearing the numerals 322—digits of great import in Bones lore. Initiates are subjected to rounds of occult hazing rituals—what pledging a fraternity might be like, perhaps, at Hogwarts. Rumors of the rites abound. Did a young Henry Luce (co-founder of TIME) actually lay naked in a coffin and tell the tales of his early sex life during his initiation? Did William F. Buckley Jr. jump into a mud pie as part of his hazing? Did any of the three Bush Bonesmen (Prescott, H.W. and W.) really receive a gift of $15,000 from the wealthy Russell Trust Association upon being tapped? The truth or falsity of all these rumors, publicized over the years by *Esquire,* the *Atlantic Monthly,* the New York *Times* and numerous independent authors, may never be known. One point that's clear: the society was men-only until the early 1990s, when women were invited to join following a heated internal debate among, uh, Bonespersons.

The Tomb has long been rumored to hold the skulls of Pancho Villa, President Martin van Buren and the Apache warrior Geronimo. If true, that's far from a laughing matter to proud Native Americans. On Feb. 17, 2009, the 100th anniversary of Geronimo's death, descendants of the Apache warrior filed a federal lawsuit against Skull and Bones, demanding that the secretive society return the skull to his family. "I believe strongly from my heart that his spirit was never released," Geronimo's great-grandson Haryln Geronimo, 61, declared at the time. Many observers believe the account that Geronimo's skull is in the Tomb is based on an old hoax. If the case moves through the courts, we may find out—and some old secrets of the Tomb may not be secret much longer.

Skull and Bones Hall

Nicknamed "the Tomb," Skull and Bones Hall, the society's headquarters in New Haven, Conn., looks as if it might have been designed by illustrator Edward Gorey. The identity of the original architect is not clear, but the addition of two towers at the rear of the building in 1911 created an enclosed courtyard that shelters outdoor Bones rites from prying eyes.

Henry Luce

The co-founder of TIME magazine, which began weekly publication in March 1923, graduated in the Yale class of 1920. As to whether he took part in the Bones practice known as "crooking," the stealing of cheap objects for a lark: TIME has no comment.

McGeorge Bundy

President Lyndon Johnson's National Security Adviser is only one of the many Skull and Bones members to have served in major roles in the U.S. government. But tales that the secretive Yale society controls Washington are best left to conspiracy theorists and thriller readers.

John Kerry

In the 2004 presidential election, both candidates were former Bonesmen, and both clung to the code of Eli omertà. "It's a secret," John Kerry, class of '66, said when asked about Bones. "So secret, I can't say anything more," George W. Bush, class of '68, wrote in his autobiography.

Bush Men

Above, a Bonesman and a legacy Bonesman sport their Yale sweaters. That's the 41st President, George H.W. Bush, holding the 43rd President, George W. Bush, circa 1946. Prescott Bush, a former U.S. Senator and the father of George H.W. Bush, is said to be the Bonesman who stole the skull of Geronimo from Fort Sill, Okla., during World War I and brought it to the Yale campus.

Bohemian Grove

"The Bohemian club! Did you say Bohemian club? That's where all those rich Republicans go up and stand naked against redwood trees, right?" The speaker was Bill Clinton; he was responding to a heckler in the crowd during a Hillary Clinton campaign event in 2007. And though the former President was joshing, he accurately summarized the public's sketchy knowledge of this highly exclusive social club, whose powerful members gather every summer at a private 2,700-acre retreat in the shade of northern California's mighty redwoods.

The male-only two-week encampment kicks off each year with an elaborate, hokey musical presentation whose theme is "The Cremation of Care." Above is one such production, a 1925 show titled *Wings*. What follows is a celebration of male bonding and networking that resembles a Sunday golf outing among executives—on steroids. A great deal of alcohol is consumed, and according to many reports, it is subsequently voided via al fresco public urination—one reason, perhaps, that President Richard Nixon, an attendee, was once caught on tape describing the Grove as "the most faggy goddamned thing you can imagine." It appears his Care failed to ignite.

Fresh air—and fresh heirs to power
Like Yale University's Skull and Bones Society, the Bohemian Grove is often credited by conspiracy theorists with possessing a grip on power far in excess of reality. But there is no denying that this bastion of wealth and power represents a privileged oligarchy, where women—and most Democrats—are not welcome. Above, at the Grove in 1967, two future Republican Presidents, Ronald Reagan (then governor of California) and Richard Nixon, about to launch his second run for the presidency, listen to the comments of Harvey Hancock, an aviation executive and GOP operative who was a longtime supporter of Nixon's political career.

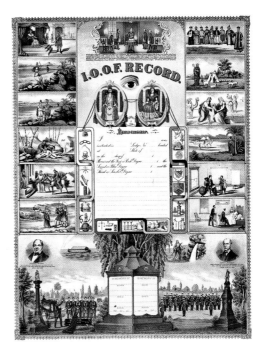

Fading Bastions of Fraternity

America is a nation of joiners, and in the 19th and 20th centuries, hundreds of fraternal organizations prospered across the country. These were not secret societies: their membership was public, and most groups had no secrets to conceal and a very public agenda to promote. But many who joined were no doubt attracted by the powerful lure of ancient lore and mystic symbols, clearly drawn from Freemasonry.

Shown above are the symbol-laden posters for two such groups, once strong in numbers, whose membership has declined over the decades. The Knights of Pythias, founded in 1864, is a fraternal order whose rites bear a strong resemblance to Masonic rituals. At its height in the early 20th century, the group dotted the U.S. with elaborate castle buildings that served as headquarters for local branches. Today it numbers some 50,000 members, far below its onetime strength. The Independent Order of Odd Fellows dates back to the 18th century; the first such groups were formed by British workers who did not belong to trade groups like the Masons and were thus "odd fellows." While there are some 200,000 remaining Odd Fellows in the U.S., the group's numbers are dwindling as its members grow older and new recruits are scarce.

Collegiate Societies

The closest many Americans ever get to joining a secret society is membership in a college fraternity or sorority. Such groups share some aspects of more traditional secret societies: exclusivity, secret balloting for entry and elaborate initiation rituals. Among the first such groups is Kappa Alpha Theta, the oldest Greek-letter fraternity for women, founded in 1870 at DePauw University in Indiana. Why "fraternity"? At Theta's birth, the term "sorority" had not yet been coined. At left, Thetas display their sistership—and millinery finery—in 1905.

Sacred space *Novelist Dan Brown's thrillers featuring symbol-sleuth Robert Langdon take place in settings rich in history and culture. Much of Angels & Demons occurs in Vatican City. Here, St. Peter's Square fills up with Roman Catholic worshippers for a Palm Sunday service in 2002. The Egyptian obelisk at right predates Christianity*

The World of Dan Brown

ANGELS & DEMONS

Novelist Dan Brown has invented a new sort of protagonist for a new sort of thriller with his unusual hero Robert Langdon, a Harvard University "symbologist." Though they feature some of the standard trappings of the form—high-tech gadgets and gizmos, a pulse-pushing pace, a female colleague/romantic interest—Brown's three Langdon novels have opened up a rich new landscape for escapist fiction, one that weds the great art and culture of the past to the mythology of secret societies and arcane knowledge. Brown's plots may demand a suspension of disbelief and his claims about the influence wielded by ancient fraternal orders may be far-fetched, but he carefully grounds his elaborate fictions in the very real streets of the world's most beautiful and historic cities.

In Brown's first Langdon novel, *Angels & Demons* (2000), readers are treated to an ongoing tutorial on the architecture and arts of Rome, the imperial city that tourists have been visiting for centuries but that Brown invites us to view with new eyes. Like Langdon, readers may find that: "It seemed Rome was suddenly filled with ellipses, pyramids, and startling geometry." In the Eternal City's streets today, tourists can be seen following in Langdon's footsteps, book in hand, eager students in the master class in symbology offered by Professors Langdon—and Brown.

CASTEL SANT'ANGELO

The approach to this imperial Roman masterpiece across the Pons Aelius (Bridge of Winds) offers a typical Dan Brown stage set: a stately promenade through beautiful artworks to a building that is rich in history, rigid in geometry and monumental in impact. The Castel was built circa A.D. 135-39 as the tomb of the Emperor Hadrian; the statue of the Archangel Michael at its summit replaced an original version sculpted by Raffaello da Montelupo in 1536.

ANGELS & DEMONS

FIRE: ST. THERESA'S PASSION

Each of the four signposts along the killer's path is devoted to one of the four primal elements of early science: earth, water, fire and air. The Chigi Chapel is associated with earth, and the murdered Cardinal Ebner is found with dirt stuffed in his mouth, a victim of suffocation. The third of the four signposts, Bernini's famous marble sculpture of the *Ecstasy of St. Theresa* in Rome's Santa Maria della Vittoria church, is associated with fire—as seen in the passion of the ecstatic nun and in the gilded shafts of light that descend from a circular window at the top of the chapel's dome that admits sunlight. Here the third victim, Cardinal Guidera of Spain, is found murdered by being incinerated alive.

Brown describes Bernini's vision of the nun's trance as portraying her "in the throes of a toe-curling orgasm"—a sexual rather than a religious experience—one of many reasons that some Catholic readers find Brown's first Langdon novel to be on the side of the demons rather than the angels.

EARTH: THE CHAPEL'S SECRET

Robert Langdon's pursuit of an assassin who is murdering four Cardinals of the Roman Catholic Church—one per hour—takes him along a "Path of Illumination" supposedly laid out in Rome by sculptor Gianlorenzo Bernini and codified by scientist Galileo Galilei. The path is a fiction, but each of its four "altars of science" is very real. The first of them, the Chigi Chapel in Rome's Santa Maria del Popolo church, features a pyramid, an age-old symbol of knowledge. On its floor is a circular image of a demon with a heralidic shield, under which Langdon discovers the body of Cardinal Ebner of Germany.

CLOCKWISE FROM TOP LEFT: ERIC VANDEVILLE—GAMMA/EYEDEA PRESSE; MASSIMO LISTRI—CORBIS; ERIC VANDEVILLE—GAMMA/EYEDEA PRESSE

WATER: A CELEBRATION OF RIVERS

Bernini's Fontana dei Quattro Fiumi in Rome's Piazza Navona was unveiled in 1651. It highlights four great rivers of the world: the Danube, Nile, Ganges and South America's Rio de la Plata. Each river is associated with an oversized statue: above is the god of the Ganges, sculpted by Bernini's student Claude Poussin: the long oar he bears is a sign of the river's navigability. The four figures form a pyramid shape around an obelisk. The ancient symbol of elevation, whose base is visible behind the sculpture, is a recurring motif in Brown's books. This fountain's obelisk, modeled after those in Egypt, was built in A.D. 81 by imperial Romans and placed here by Bernini. In Brown's novel, Langdon comes close to saving the fourth victim of the killer, Cardinal Baggia of Italy, but the prelate drowns at this fourth "altar of science," clearly associated with water.

AIR: A SUBTLE SIGNPOST

This bas-relief embedded in the stones of St. Peter's Square in Vatican City is the second of the four "altars of science"; it is associated with the air. Here the killer's second victim is found: Cardinal Lamassé of France died after his lungs were punctured.

COLLIDER-SCOPE

In Dan Brown's world, the Large
Hadron Collider (LHC) at the
European Organization for Nuclear
Research (CERN) facility outside
Geneva shares the "fearful symmetry"
that William Blake discerned in a
tiger. The facility, the world's foremost
laboratory for subatomic research,
indeed produces small quantities of
antimatter, the MacGuffin that drives
the plot of *Angels & Demons.* But the
lab has been so pestered with inquiries
by readers of Brown's book that it
now offers an FAQ on its website, in
which it explains that "in 1995 CERN
became the first laboratory to create
anti-atoms artificially." However, say
the scientists at the Organisation
Européen pour la Recherche
Nucléaire, it is not possible at this time
to store a large amount of the stuff.

How large is the Large Hadron
Collider? Its circular underground
loop is some 17 miles (27 km) in
circumference, crossing the border
from Switzerland into France at an
average depth of 328 ft. (100 m). When
the largest scientific instrument in
history went online in September
2008 after 15 years of development
and $10 billion in expense, it broke
down due to the overheating of
two magnets. It went live again,
successfully, on Nov. 30, 2009.

MAXIMILIEN BRICE—CERN/GAMMA/EYEDEA PRESSE

THE DA VINCI CODE

Just as Rome is the featured city and Bernini the presiding artist of Dan Brown's *Angels & Demons,* Paris and Leonardo da Vinci are the dominant location and genius of 2003's *The Da Vinci Code.* The novel begins and ends at the Louvre Museum, where architect I.M. Pei's magnificent glass pyramid dominates the courtyard of the former royal palace, its shape echoed in an inverted form beneath the plaza. *The Da Vinci Code* propelled Brown to the top of the best-seller lists and made Robert Langdon a superstar. By 2009 it had sold an estimated 80 million copies, while the 2006 film version had brought in $758.2 million at the worldwide box office.

Although the novel is propelled by a gripping plot that takes place within a 24-hour period, it is the book's controversial subject matter that made it a global cause célèbre. In the course of the novel, the symbologist Langdon discovers a plot 20 centuries old to conceal the fact that Jesus Christ was married to Mary Magdalene and that their offspring still survive. This sort of notion had been advanced before but had attracted little attention from the general public, and its use as a plot device, even in what is no more than a fictional thriller, deeply offended many Christian readers.

THE LOUVRE PYRAMID

Architect Pei's glass structure towers 69 ft. (21 m) over the courtyard of the Louvre. Denounced by many as an affront to the museum's classic design when it was unveiled in 1989, the grid of transparent diamonds has now become one of the world's most recognizable landmarks. The pyramid form is regarded as a signpost of illumination by students of mystical geometry.

SECRETS OF AN ANCIENT SUPPER

With his love of codes and secrets and his brilliance as artist and thinker, Leonardo da Vinci might well have sprung full-blown from the brain of Dan Brown. But this restless polymath—history's original Renaissance man—was a very real figure, whose visionary experiments in metallurgy, aviation, engineering and a gaggle of other topics are clearly the work of an inspired genius. As the title of Brown's second Robert Langdon novel reveals, it is Leonardo in his role as codifier and keeper of mysteries that intrigues the author. "Da Vinci was a prankster," Langdon claims, and in the novel, important secrets are hidden both in his paintings and in so-called cryptexes, intricate repositories supposedly designed by Leonardo to destroy their contents if not opened by those able to decipher subtle clues to their operation.

The revelation that drives the plot of *The Da Vinci Code* is found within one of Leonardo's most famous works: his well-known mural of the *Last Supper* of Christ and his disciples, which the artist painted on a wall of the convent church of Santa Maria delle Grazie, Milan, completing the work in 1498. Langdon claims that the figure immediately to the left of Christ (from the viewer's perspective) is not the disciple John, as long believed, but rather Mary Magdalene, Christ's secret bride. Whether readers buy into this argument or not, there is no denying the feminine aspect of the individual depicted in Leonardo's 15 ft.-by-29 ft. (4.5 m by 8.8 m) masterpiece.

MAN, THE MEASURE OF ALL THINGS

Leonardo's fascinating depiction of the human body as a repository of geometric forms is the opening image of *The Da Vinci Code.* The name of the piece is an homage to the great Roman scholar of architecture Vitruvius, who argued that the proportions of classical buildings reflect the lineaments of the human body. Much to the distress of the world's art historians, Brown portrays Leonardo in the book as a practitioner of "spiritual hypocrisy," who painted masterpieces of Christian symbolism "purely as a commercial venture." Yet much to the delight of the world's thriller readers, Brown appropriates Leonardo's late 1400s sketch in an elegant manner: the murdered curator of the Louvre assumes the famous form in his dying moments, using his own body as a symbolic clue to his killer's identity.

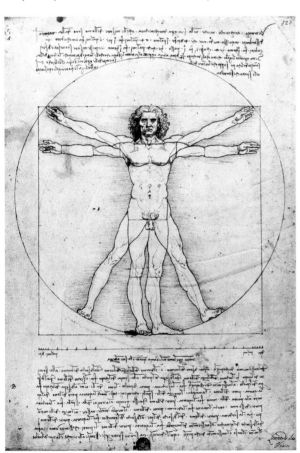

DIVIDING LINES

After *The Da Vinci Code* was published, so many tourists clogged Paris' church of Saint-Sulpice to see its "rose line" that authorities refused to allow the church to appear in the film of the book. In the novel's fanciful account, the brass line in the floor of the nave that leads to a tall gnomon, above, is the "Prime Meridian line of Paris," or "rose line," a name associated with Rosslyn Chapel in Scotland, reputed home to the Holy Grail. In reality, the line and gnomon were put in place in 1743 by church prelates as a sundial, oriented so that sunlight falls on the line on the year's equinoxes and solstices.

The Da Vinci Code includes so many fascinating—but false—statements about Saint-Sulpice that church authorities placed a poster in the church, correcting several of the book's assertions: that Saint-Sulpice was once a pagan temple; that its brass line and gnomon mark the obsolete meridian; and that the letters *P* and *S* in the chuch's stained-glass windows stand for "Priory of Sion," an organization supposedly devoted to preserving the bloodline of Christ. Brown did not invent this nonexistent group: a French aristocrat and pretender to the throne, Pierre Plantard, created this faux society in the 1950s as an exercise in historical surrealism.

ROSSLYN CHAPEL

Rosslyn Chapel was built in the mid–15th century by Scottish nobleman William St. Clair, whose family was descended from Norman knights and was close to Scotland's royal family. The structure in the Midlothian region has long been the subject  of legends and myths, largely because its walls and floors are as thickly encrusted with ornately wrought mystical emblems as ... well, as the pages of a Dan Brown novel. The chapel has come to be associated with both the Knights Templar and Freemasonry; Rosslyn is a sort of Roswell for seekers of the Holy Grail. No connection with the Knights Templar has been proved, but several members of the St. Clair family became high-ranking Masons in the centuries after the chapel was built. The structure plays a crucial role in *The Da Vinci Code,* where it is depicted as the home of the offspring of Jesus Christ; in the fictitious theology of the novel, the Grail is the divine bloodline of Christ, as carried in Mary Magdalene, who is the vessel of his descendants.

In 2006, scientists from the Glasgow School of Art and the governmental preservation group Historic Scotland began exploring the chapel using a method Robert Langdon might envy: they trained high-powered lasers on the structure. Registering some 50,000 points in space each second, the laser beams documented its most minute details, yielding a 3-D model of it, right, that is accurate to millimeters. The laser scans clearly reveal the underground crypt at the rear of the chapel, whose doors have long been locked and which is reputed by some to be the repository of the Grail. The bound, inverted angel on one corbel, shown at top right, represents the fallen Lucifer. The carved head of a "Green Man" at the far top right is an ancient symbol of renewal and fertility.

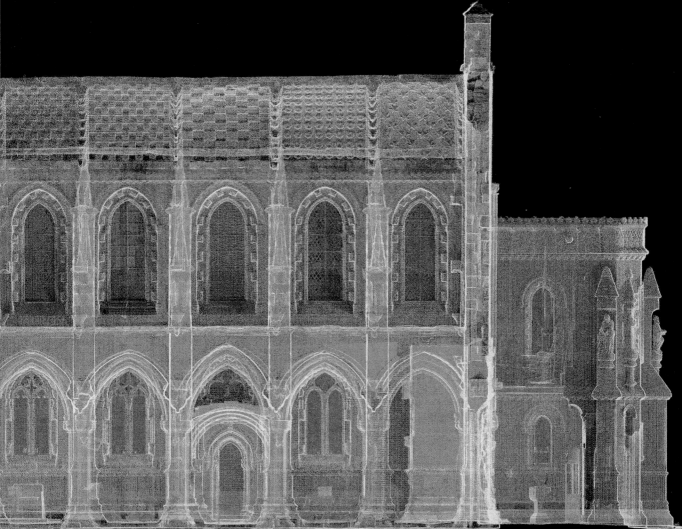

THE LOST SYMBOL

For his third Robert Langdon thriller, Dan Brown decided to give his passport a rest—and give himself a tough assignment. As TIME book critic Lev Grossman reported, "Brown has another agenda in *The Lost Symbol,* which is to rehabilitate Washington, D.C., as one of the great world capitals of gothic mystery, one that can hold its own with Paris or London or Rome … He's set himself a huge challenge. What he did for Christianity in *Angels & Demons* and *The Da Vinci Code,* Brown is now trying to do for America: reclaim its richness, its darkness, its weirdness." Indeed, one of the virtues of looking at the world through the eyes of Langdon is that he makes us see marvelous new aspects of landmarks whose power has been sapped by familiarity. Monumental Washington, readers of *The Lost Symbol* find, is a treasure trove of architectural and cultural symbols that have been waiting to be reanimated by Brown.

When the last page is turned on the book, Brown's fans are free to indulge in what has become an enjoyable guessing game: Which city and which shadowy cultural forces will Brown choose for Langdon's next adventures? One clue: three months after the release of *The Lost Symbol,* Brown was spotted at the 2009 opening-night gala performance of Milan's famed La Scala opera house. Regarding the horseshoe-shaped auditorium and its six gilded balconies, Brown told reporters, "Somebody clearly needs to fall." Game on!

A PRESIDENTIAL DEITY?

The Lost Symbol takes full advantage of the majesty of the monuments of Washington, D.C. The plot begins with the finding of the severed hand of a powerful museum director and Mason near the statue of George Washington in the Rotunda of the U.S. Capitol building. The mural on the dome, *The Apotheosis of Washington,* shows the first President ascending to immortality. It was painted in 1865 by Constantino Brumidi.

MASONIC SHRINE

A pair of sphinxes stand guard at the entrance to the House of the Temple, the headquarters of the Scottish Rite of Freemasonry, Southern Jurisdiction, Washington, D.C. Designed by John Russell Pope as an homage to the Tomb of Mausolus, one of the seven wonders of the ancient world, the building was completed in 1915. It is the setting for both the prologue and climax of *The Lost Symbol*. Pope left his Classical Revival stamp on the capital; his other designs include the Jefferson Memorial and National Archives.

WASHINGTON'S TEMPLE

The U.S. was founded in a revolt against royal authority and the divine right of kings—so visitors to the George Washington Masonic Memorial in Alexandria, Va., *(above)* may be surprised by the trappings of sanctity surrounding this monument to the first President. The structure is "as impressive as any building on the National Mall," according to one of Brown's characters.

MAZE OF MURALS

The Library of Congress building *(left)* was designed in a flamboyant Beaux Arts style; the Romanesque arches in its Great Hall resemble an M.C. Escher drawing. Completed in 1897, the building was renamed the Thomas Jefferson Building in 1980, honoring Jefferson's original donations to the first Library of Congress. Its grand interior spaces are home to ornate murals and lavish sculptures and ornaments.

A GOTHIC INVADER ON CLASSICAL TURF

In a city whose primary design influences are Roman, Greek and Egyptian, Washington National Cathedral offers a contrast: it is executed in High Gothic style, bringing stained-glass windows, flying buttresses, glaring gargoyles *(right)* and a surplus of spires to the capital. Seat of the presiding bishop of the U.S. Episcopal Church, it was begun in 1909 and completed in 1990. Some Masons claim its altar is made of stone taken from the same Jerusalem quarry where the blocks in Solomon's Temple are believed to have been mined.

FACING PAGE: PIXTAL—AGE FOTOSTOCK; THIS PAGE: NOAH ADDIS—STAR LEDGER/CORBIS

AMERICAN OBELISKS

Since the days of the ancient Egyptians, obelisks—plinths topped with pyramids—have been regarded as emblems of mankind's striving for enlightenment. Small wonder two monuments dedicated to George Washington around the nation's capital city assume this ancient form.

At far left is the George Washington Masonic Memorial in Alexandria, Va., designed by New York City architects Helmle & Corbett. The exterior was completed in 1932 and the interior in 1970. It is modeled after ancient Egypt's famed lighthouse of Alexandria, and its three ascending rows of increasingly elaborate columns trace the evolution of Greek style from Doric to Ionic to Corinthian modes.

TOWERS TOPPED WITH LIGHT

At near left is the Washington Monument, which anchors one end of the National Mall, forming a triangle with the White House and the U.S. Capitol. Designed by Robert Mills, a Freemason, in the 1840s but not completed until 1884, it stands 555 ft. 5⅛ in. (169.294 m) and is the tallest obelisk in the world, as well as the tallest structure in Washington, D.C. Freemasons hosted a lavish celebration observing the laying of the cornerstone of the tower on July 4, 1848.

The photograph is laden with Masonic symbolism, echoing the shape of the plinth and orb of light that are prominent symbols in the society's lore. Movie fans will recall a similar geometric arrangement in Stanley Kubrick's film *2001: A Space Odyssey,* when the appearance of the sun over a black monolith heralds a transforming moment of enlightenment for the human race. In similar fashion, the George Washington Masonic Memorial building is topped with a permanent, stylized flame. For another iteration of this visual theme—a vertical shaft topped with circular illumination—look back at the statue of Washington in the U.S. Capitol, outlined against the building's radiant inner dome.

The Face of the Modern Thriller

In Dan Brown's shotgun-wedding novels, the potboiler hooks up with the humanities seminar

Ever harbor a secret urge to assume the role of Robert Langdon? Readers of Dan Brown's novels featuring the Harvard University "symbologist" know the drill by heart: get up each morning at 4 and do 50 laps in a university pool, the better to maintain your former varsity swimmer's physique. Then don your unvarying outfit: khakis, Harris Tweed blazer, cordovan loafers—and don't forget the Mickey Mouse watch, a gift from your father, and the tip-off that your approach to the world makes room for whimsy.

For those who'd prefer to trade places with Langdon's creator and become a wealthy writer of immensely popular thrillers, the regimen is remarkably similar. Get up early each morning and dive into your writing chores by 4, when your mind is clear. Keep track of your progress via an antique hourglass, an emblem of your love affair with the heritage of the past. Make sure to delete a hefty amount of your first efforts: self-editing is the key to success, Brown believes. And when you get stumped, put on your gravity boots and hang upside down for a spell; it's a great way to shift your perspective, according to the novelist.

Above all, don't forget the gift from your father. Brown's dad Richard was a teacher of mathematics at the exclusive Phillips Exeter Academy in Exeter, N.H., and he was a lover of games and puzzles, a solver of crosswords and anagrams whose Christmas gifts to his three children often took the form of elaborate treasure hunts—yes, exactly the sort of puzzle-plagued mad dash that is the driving plot mechanism of every Robert Langdon book.

Brown's path to the creation of Langdon was more leisurely. After graduating from Amherst College in 1986, he set out to become a singer-songwriter. His mother, a musician, served as choirmaster at an Episcopal church in Exeter. Brown's dreams led him to Southern California, where he did some teaching and concentrated on his musical efforts. But the namesake CD *Dan Brown* in 1993 and the next year's *Angels & Demons* (you can't make this stuff up, folks) failed to make a splash—even though the second album's cover art featured an ambigram for its title, which Brown later used in his first Langdon novel. That ambigram, a word designed to be read both right-side-up and upside down, was designed by graphic artist John Langdon; Brown later saluted the

Every which way
This ambigram of the word Illuminati *was created by graphic artist John Langdon for* Angels & Demons

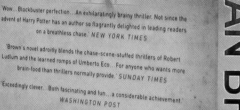

Who, me? *Brown poses for a portrait in Exeter, N.H., his boyhood home and current residence. Reticent and preppy, he prefers to keep a low profile. "'I'm just a guy who tells a story," he has insisted in multiple interviews*

designer by naming his fictional hero after him (repeat: we are not making this up).

If Brown's music failed to catch fire, something else did: Blythe Newlon, who worked at the National Academy of Songwriters, became a friend, then a supporter and business adviser who strongly promoted Brown's musical career, and finally, despite being 12 years older than Brown, his wife.

In 1993, the pair moved to New Hampshire, where Brown returned to the Phillips Exeter Academy as an English teacher. His eureka moment occurred while vacationing on the island of Tahiti in 1994, when he picked up a copy of Sidney Sheldon's novel *The Doomsday Conspiracy* and decided, "Hey, I can do that." The result was a cyberthriller set primarily in Spain titled *Digital Fortress*. Published in 1998, it was a minor success, as was the similar *Deception Point,* published in 2001. For both books, Blythe Brown again served as an informal marketing director, lining up bookstore appearances and handling other publicity chores.

While writing his novels, Brown also collaborated with his wife on books of humor; he now credits her with being the chief researcher on his history-saturated

Langdon novels and with playing a major role in their creation. Robert Langdon was introduced to the reading public in 2000 in *Angels & Demons.* But as with Brown's two other early thrillers, the book was published in a small edition and didn't make the best-seller lists. Yet Brown believed that he had struck a rich vein of material to draw on with his Harvard prof, and he began working on a second Langdon novel.

Angels & Demons is set largely in Vatican City, and Brown reveled in its Roman Catholic mise-en-scène, featuring scenes set in the Pope's private apartment, treasure hunts in the Vatican Secret Archives and all the panoply of a papal election. The new novel, *The Da Vinci Code,* again dug into church history and centered on the highly provocative premise that Jesus Christ had fathered a child by Mary Magdalene, and that this bloodline had survived into the present. This notion, while not original, was little known to most readers, and Brown's new publisher took full advantage of its possibilities to create controversy. Taking a risk, Doubleday printed 100,000 copies in its first press run, promoted the novel fever-

Langdon by the Numbers
Dan Brown's three novels featuring Robert Langdon are one of the greatest success stories in publishing history. Critics may carp, but the reading public votes at the cash register

Angels & Demons
- **Published:** May, 2000
- **First printing:** 25,000 copies
- **Sales as of January 2010:** 39 million copies, and counting
- **Film version:** released 2009. Worldwide box office as of January, 2010: $486 million
- **Publishing history:** *Angels & Demons* is one of those novels, beloved of publishers, that sells poorly on first publication but later takes off in the back draft created by the huge success of later titles in a franchise series. *Angels* profited from two boosts, first when *The Da Vinci Code* became a worldwide sensation and then, six years later, when tie-in copies were released to coincide with the debut of the film version in May, 2009.

The Da Vinci Code
- **Published:** March, 2003
- **First printing:** 100,000 copies
- **Sales as of January 2010:** 81 million copies, and counting
- **Film version:** released 2006. Worldwide box office as of January, 2010: $758 million
- **Critical response:**

Salman Rushdie: "A novel so bad that it gives bad novels a bad name."

Stephen King: "The intellectual equivalent of Kraft Macaroni and Cheese."

Janet Maslin, the *New York Times*: "The author is Dan Brown (a name you will want to remember). In this gleefully erudite suspense novel, Mr. Brown takes the format he has been developing through three earlier novels and fine-tunes it to blockbuster perfection. Not since the advent of Harry Potter has an author so flagrantly delighted in leading readers on a breathless chase and coaxing them through hoops ... this author is drawn to the place where empirical evidence and religious faith collide. And he creates a bracing exploration of this realm ... The book moves at a breakneck pace, with the author seeming thoroughly to enjoy his contrivances."

The Lost Symbol
- **Published:** September 2009
- **First printing:** 6.5 million copies
- **Sales as of January 2010:** 19 million copies in print, and counting
- **Film version:** Scheduled for release in 2012, subject to change
- **Critical response:**

Lev Grossman, TIME: "The plot of *The Lost Symbol* churns forward with a brutalist energy that makes character but a flesh appendage on its iron machine. It's fun, but you feel a bit bruised afterward."

Janet Maslin, the New York Times: "... bringing sexy back to a genre that had been left for dead ... impossible to put down ... [Brown] uses so many italics that even *brilliant experts* wind up sounding like *teenage girls* ... [yet] his excitable, hyperbolic tone is one of the guilty pleasures of his books: ('Actually, Katherine, it's not gibberish.' His eyes brightened again with the thrill of discovery. 'It's ... Latin.')"

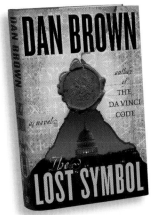

ishly and reaped the rewards when it entered the best-seller list at No. 1 on its publication in March 2003.

Ka-boom! Surfing on a wave of controversy, *The Da Vinci Code* became one of the most talked-about books in memory. Readers devoured it, enjoying both its pulse-pounding plot and its newfangled hero, whose operative terrain turned the hitherto brainless airplane read into a stimulating intellectual adventure. The book spawned *Code*-themed dinners in Kentucky, art museum seminars in Utah, popular tours of the churches and museums of Paris, websites and books devoted to nailing any and all inaccuracies in the text—even other best sellers refuting its premise.

Around the world, and especially in Europe, Christians and devout Roman Catholics were deeply offended by the book's provocative premise: copies were burned, and protests were held. But as p.r. experts like to say, there is no such thing as bad publicity, and the ruckus just kept driving sales. By 2005, the *Code* had sold 25 million copies. In a predictable next act, Hollywood beckoned, Tom Hanks starred, critics panned but fans shelled out—and a film franchise was born.

Brown's critics aren't confined to movie reviewers. The Langdon novels have been blasted for Brown's clunky, breathless prose, by TIME's critics and many others, including, oddly, even fans of the books. The consensus: he's no Nabokov, but then again, the Beach Boys aren't Bach, and we need both.

Brown's challenge following the *Da Vinci Code's* success is the sort of task familiar to Pablo Picasso or the Beatles: How on earth could he top himself? The success of the *Code* left him "temporarily crippled," he told *Parade* magazine. The New York *Times* helpfully spelled out the stakes: "Could he still tell a breathless treasure-hunt story? Could he lard it with weirdly illuminating minutiae? Could he turn some form of profound wisdom into a pretext for escapist fun?" Result: Brown took six years to deliver his next Langdon escapade, *The Lost Symbol,* a story of Masonic intrigue set in Washington.

Symbol, as anticipated, initially sold like hotcakes on its publication in September 2009, but hopes of sales-stimulating controversy were dashed when most Masons embraced it. It's possible the novel may sell "only" 25-30 million copies—and that's why would-be Dan Browns should realize they have some very big gravity boots to fill. ■

On trial *Dan Brown testified in London in 2006 when French authors Michael Baigent and Richard Leigh filed a plagiarism suit accusing him of having lifted the main thesis of* The Da Vinci Code *from their 1982 work,* The Holy Blood and the Holy Grail.

Brown won a resounding victory; British judge Peter Smith even encoded a cryptic message in his decision

The Cinema of Symbology
TIME critic Richard Corliss takes the measure of the two film adaptations of the Robert Langdon novels. Coming to a theater near you in 2012: *The Lost Symbol*

Tom Hanks as Langdon; Audrey Tautou as Sophie Nevue

A Cardinal's death by fire

The Da Vinci Code (2006)

Everybody but Dan Brown knows that *The Da Vinci Code* is not a great book; at best it's a great read. But for all the novel's thriller tropes, its chases among chalices and cilices, the publishing phenomenon of the decade is a very bookish book. The games Brown plays are essentially literary: anagrams and hexagrams, fun with the Fibonacci Sequence. Those riddles are best savored by readers with a long night or a long flight ahead of them. They are not, however, intrinsically visual or dramatic. To make a real movie out of *The Da Vinci Code* requires a rethinking of the book. Or at least a thinking. Instead, director Ron Howard and screenwriter Akiva Goldsman pounded out a faithful synopsis and filmed it. The result is a work that is politically brave, for a mainstream movie, and artistically stodgy.

The plot—about the pursuit of a Harvard professor (Tom Hanks) and a French policewoman (Audrey Tautou) by a devout, albino hit man (Paul Bettany) and rival gangs of learned loonies, all in search of Christ's Holy Grail—has some superficial bustle, but essentially it's a course in speculative religious and art history. Somebody talks, the others listen. Those lectures give most of the actors little to do. Ian McKellen, as a crotchety charmer, fares best, because he does most of the talking. Bettany comes in second.

The bravery? Filming and financing what, if the story is taken seriously, is a corrosive challenge to Christianity. But having made the bold decision to film the novel, Howard hasn't the energy to slap the thing to life. He's like a guide on one of the countless *Da Vinci Code* tours of Paris or London, doing it by rote, letting the film hobble to its climax with still more exposition. Good movies are show-and-tell; this one is all-tell, no-show.

Angels & Demons (2009)

Cinematically, Ron Howard's *The Da Vinci Code* was a slog. But it soon became the 27th top worldwide grosser in film history, so here comes *Angels:* same star (Tom Hanks), director (Ron Howard), producer (Brian Grazer) and scripter (Akiva Goldsman, abetted this time by David Koepp). Also the same approach: it's a movie, so we'd better feign movement. The back-history in which Langdon is an expert requires Hanks to speak dialogue with its own footnotes, so Howard camouflages the static nature of the enterprise by having his star spout arcana while rushing from church to church. In fact, virtually all the actors have to talk the talk while they walk the walk. When they take a breather and stand still, the camera skates 360s around them.

As transparent as this device is, *Angels* has elemental satisfactions in its blend of movie genres that could appeal to wide segments of the audience. For Hollywood's core demographic, this is a serial-killer thriller, not far from the *Saw* series in its devoutly clinical depiction of distressed bodies. (See the eyeball on the floor! Gasp as plump rats snack on a dead Cardinal's face!) For adults, the movie is a backstage story of Vatican politicking that paints the College of Cardinals as possibly the only ruling body older and more removed from mundane realities than the U.S. Supreme Court.

Some of the cast members are given room to create plausible characters, which helps compensate for the cipher at the center. Not that Hanks is bad; there's just no person for him to portray. It's a shame that Langdon doesn't play to his strengths: the fretfulness and impatience that rise to heroism. Here he's a simple conduit for information, the docent on our tour of Roman churches.

Creeds in Hiding

A private world *Walled off from U.S. society, the compound and temple of the renegade Mormon sect the Fundamentalist Church of Jesus Christ of Latter Day Saints rise starkly from the desert outside Eldorado, Texas.*

The Gospel Truth?

Modern scholars remake the image of Mary Magdalene

Summer page-turners generally sidestep the finer points of 6th century church history. Or they did until Dan Brown enlisted Mary Magdalene to drive the plot of *The Da Vinci Code*. In basing his tale around this complex figure, he chose a character whose actual identity is in play, both in theology and pop culture. Three decades ago, the Roman Catholic Church quietly admitted what critics had been saying for centuries: Mary's standard image as a reformed prostitute is not supported by the text of the Bible. Freed of this lurid, limiting premise and employing varying ratios of scholarship and whimsy, academics and enthusiasts have begun positing various other Marys: a rich and honored patron of Jesus, an Apostle in her own right, the mother of the Messiah's child and even his prophetic successor.

The wealth of possibilities has inspired a wave of literature, both academic and popular. And it has gained Mary a new following among Catholics who see in her a potent female role model and a possible argument against the all-male priesthood. The woman who three Gospels agree was the first witness to Christ's Resurrection is having her own kind of rebirth.

Centuries of Catholic teaching established Mary's colloquial identity as the bad girl who became the hope of all bad girls, the saved siren active not only in the overheated imaginations of parochial-school students but also as the patron of institutions for wayward women such as the grim nun-run laundries featured in the 2003 movie *The Magdalene Sisters.* (The word *maudlin* derives from Mary's reputation as a tearful penitent.)

The only problem is that it turns out that she wasn't bad, she was just interpreted that way. Mary Magdalene (her name refers to Magdala, a city in Galilee) first appears in the Gospel of Luke as one of several apparently wealthy women Jesus cures of possession (seven demons are cast from her), who join him and the Apostles and "provided for them out of their means." Her name does not come up again until the Crucifixion, which she and other women witness from the foot of the cross, the male disciples having fled. On Easter Sunday morning, she visits Jesus' sepulcher, either alone or with other women, and discovers it empty. She learns—in three Gospels from angels and in one from Jesus himself— that he is risen. The net impression is of a woman of substance, brave and smart and devoted, who plays a crucial role in Christianity's defining moment.

So where did all the juicy stuff come from? Mary's image became distorted when early church leaders bundled into her story those of several less distinguished women whom the Bible did not name or referred to without a last name. The mix-up was made official by Pope Gregory the Great in 591, although the teaching was not adopted by Orthodox or Protestant

In the 16th century, Italian master Titian painted Mary Magdalene with bare breasts, a sign of her sexual license.

Judas Iscariot, far left, is another New Testament figure in transition. The Gospel of Judas, an alleged Coptic Egyptian transcript of a 2nd century Gnostic text, was unveiled in 2006. Its provocative premise: Judas is a sympathetic figure who was Christ's closest associate

theologians when each of these branches of Christianity later split from Catholicism.

In 1969, in the liturgical equivalent of fine print, the Catholic church officially separated Mary from her fallen sisters as part of a general revision of its missal. And her rehabilitation has been buttressed by other recent scholarship. Historians of Christianity (and the readers of Dan Brown novels) are increasingly fascinated with a group of early followers of Christ known broadly as the Gnostics, who wrote gospels not included in the official New Testament. And the Gnostics were fascinated by Mary. The so-called Gospel of Mary [Magdalene], which may date from as early as A.D. 125 (or about 40 years after John's Gospel), describes her as having received a private vision from Jesus, which she then passed on to the male disciples. That amounts to a usurpation of the go-between status the standard Gospels normally accord to St. Peter, the disciple named by Christ as his successor and from whom Popes trace their authority. Small wonder, some feminist scholars trace Mary's depiction by the church as a fallen woman to a long-forgotten gender battle. Now, 14 centuries later: Behold—She is risen! ∎

The Secrets Of Opus Dei

Does this mysterious order create brainwashed zealots—or simply forge a deeper form of faith?

Whack! Moviegoers will long remember the scene in the 2006 film version of Dan Brown's thriller *The Da Vinci Code* in which a grim-faced fellow utters Christ's name repeatedly and then—smack!—whales away at his already bloodied back with an Inquisition-issue cat-o'-nine-tails. The self-inflicted ordeal of the albino assassin Silas, a fanatical member of a Roman Catholic group called Opus Dei, sealed this lay society's reputation as a powerful, ultraconservative faction of the church riddled with sadomasochistic ritual.

Brown stated the portrayal was "based on numerous books written about Opus Dei as well as on my own personal interviews." Yet in casting the group as his heavy, Brown was as shrewd as someone setting up an innocent man for a crime. You don't choose the head of the Rotary; you single out the secretive guy at the end of the block with the off-putting tics, who perhaps has a couple of incidents in his past that will hinder an effective defense. And that's not a bad sketch of Opus Dei. In its 82 years, this society founded by a young Spanish priest has been a rumor magnet. Successful and secretive, it

has been accused of using lavish riches and carefully cultivated clout to do everything from propping up Francisco Franco's Spanish dictatorship to pushing through founder Josemaría Escrivá's premature sainthood to encouraging self-abuse.

In response to the film's over-the-top portrayal, Opus Dei officials took the offensive, breaking their organization's historical silence. In 2006 they spoke at length on record to John Allen, a respected print and television Vatican commentator, and offered him unprecedented access to Opus Dei records and personnel. He responded with *Opus Dei: An Objective Look Behind the Myths and Reality of the Most Controversial Force in the Catholic Church* (Doubleday), probably the most informed and sympathetic treatment of the group ever penned by an outsider.

But the 2006 public relations offensive never quite managed to close the gap between what critics say Opus is about and its own self-portrait. On one side there is "Octopus Dei," or, as *Harper's* magazine once put it, "an authoritarian and semi-clandestine enterprise that manages to infiltrate its indoctrinated technocrats, politicos and administrators into the highest levels of the state." On the other is the portrait

A mission shared
Devout members of Opus Dei mortify their bodies to ensure humility and share Christ's and the world's pain. Tools used include a small rope lash, top, called a "discipline," and a cilice, a barbed chain worn on the thigh.

At right, a shrine in Rome's Basilica of San Eugenio honors Opus Dei founder Josemaría Escrivá

VAE DVORVM PRINCIPVM ES CONSECRATA GLORI

A modern saint
Opus Dei founder Josemaría Escrivá addresses a rapt crowd in Barcelona in 1972. After his death in 1975 at 73, Pope John Paul II, a longtime admirer, put the Spanish priest on a fast track for sainthood and canonized him in 2002

of this world. They bend Opus' daily two hours of religious observance around a more typical (or perhaps retro, given the large size of many of their families) existence.

For all its uniqueness in mission and structure, Opus Dei is best known for being secretive. It has a special set of greetings: *"Pax"* and *"In aeternum"* ("Peace" and "In eternity"). Its 1950 constitution barred members from revealing their membership without permission from the director of their center. In 1982 a new document repudiated "secrecy or clandestine activity," yet Opus will still not identify its members, and many prefer not to identify themselves. Nor, as Allen showed in his book, will Opus formally own up to many of its institutions. Its U.S. schools tend to go by bland names like the Heights and Northridge Prep. For years, he reports, the 17-story U.S. headquarters in New York City, finished in 2001, lacked an identifying street-level sign.

The normal assumption about such indirectness would be that the group is hiding something, and filthy lucre is a staple of the Opus myth. Two rumors about its popularity with Pope John Paul II are that it funded the Solidarity trade union and helped bail out the Vatican bank after a 1982 scandal. Poverty is not one of Opus' vows. In 2006, Allen estimated, there was $344.4 million in Opus assets in the U.S. and a global total of $2.8 billion—a handsome sum but hardly Vatican bailout money. Besides, what most intrigues the public isn't the cash—it's the lash.

painted by Opus' U.S. vicar, Thomas Bohlin, who in 2006 sat for several hours with TIME for an interview. Opus, he explained, is just a teaching entity, a kind of advanced school for intense Catholic spiritual growth with minimal global coordination or input as to how members apply what they learn.

Yet Opus Dei is far from a kind of spiritual pick-me-up for casual Catholics. It features a small, highly committed membership (87,000 worldwide and a mere 3,000 in the U.S.). Members take part in a rigorous course of spiritual "formation" that stresses church doctrine and contemplation as well as Escrivá's philosophy of work and personal holiness. Opus' core is its "numeraries," the 20% who, despite remaining lay, pledge celibacy, live together in one of about 1,700 sex-segregated "centers"—all while holding day jobs, with most of their pay devolving to the group. That near cloistered life produces the group's most avid, satisfied members and its bitterest dropouts. Some 70% of the membership, called supernumeraries, are much more

The man doing penance advised his associate to cover his head with a blanket, but the observer could not stop his ears. "Soon," said the witness, "I began to hear the forceful blows of his discipline … there were more than a thousand terrible blows, precisely timed. The floor was covered in blood." That is not an early *Da Vinci Code* draft. It is a description of Opus Dei founder Escrivá's routine by his eventual successor, quoted in a biography of Escrivá. Escrivá emphasized that others should not emulate his ferocity. But numeraries are expected, although not compelled, to wear a cilice, a small chain with inward-pointing spikes, around the upper thigh for two hours each day, and to flail themselves briefly each week with a small rope lash (rather than Silas's jumbo whip) called a "discipline."

With rare exceptions, even defectors don't cite self-mortification, as it's known, as their deal killer. One former numerary assistant told TIME it was "nothing. It's not like *The Da Vinci Code*." Catholic laity and luminaries, including Mother Teresa, have employed the practice. San Antonio Archbishop José Gomez, an Opus member, notes self-mortification's tie to Opus' roots: "In the Hispanic culture," he says, "you look at the crucifixes, and they have a lot of blood. We are more used to sacrifice in the sense of physical suffering."

Self-mortification resonates with critics because, as Allen points out, it provides a metaphor for what they see as an "inhumane approach within Opus Dei, which demands a kind of dominance over its members, body and soul." Unnerving stories have been passed by ex-numeraries to journalists or posted to the anti-Opus website *odan. org*. Many involve charges of deceptive recruiting, with prospective members unaware that the events they are invited to are Opus', of numeraries' realizing only belatedly that Opus expects them to sign away their paycheck and curtail relations with their families. The music they play and the publications they read are allegedly controlled, and they must report their own and others' deviations as part of a system of "fraternal correction." Center directors are portrayed as little dictators. Complaining to local bishops is futile because of Opus' semi-independent status.

Opus responds that those who leave are a small minority, and Allen describes the mood around the many centers he visited as cheerful. Bohlin dismisses charges that prospective members are unaware of what to expect, pointing out that all go through an 18-month preparatory process. "I don't believe Opus Dei is either a [cult] or a mafia or a cabal," a senior prelate of another religious community in Rome told TIME. It is just that "their approach is preconciliar. They originated prior to the Second Vatican Council, and they don't want to dialogue with society as they find it." That would not describe the majority of today's self-identifying American Catholics, who are distinctly postconciliar, with more than 75% opposing the birth-control ban. But it may jibe with the views of tomorrow's flock, if, as seems likely, U.S. Catholicism becomes more Hispanic and more conservative in the decades ahead. ∎

Opus Dei, Now and Then

On Oct. 2, 1928, a 26-year-old Spanish priest named Josemaría Escrivá was visited by a new vision of Catholic spirituality: a movement of pious laypeople who would, by prayerful contemplation and the dedication of their labor to Christ, extend the holiness of church on Sunday into their everyday work life. Escrivá called his order Opus Dei—"the Work of God."

Current leader Echeverría

The society was controversial almost from birth. Opus threatened the era's Catholic clericalism, which privileged priests, monks and nuns over the laity, and Escrivá was called a heretic by some. For decades, prominent Opus Dei members served in dictator Francisco Franco's church-supportive regime in Spain, sparking ongoing speculation about the group's conservative political leanings.

Escrivá himself was a polarizing figure, humble and grandiose, avuncular and ferocious. His order grew slowly but steadily, remaining below the radar of most Catholics. That all changed in 1982, when Pope John Paul II granted Escrivá's wish that Opus be a "personal prelature," able in some cases to leapfrog local archbishops and deal directly with Rome—a position of papal favor similar to that once granted the Knights Templar. The order's ecclesiastical power was shown by Escrivá's 1992 beatification, a brief 17 years after his death; 10 years later, 300,000 people thronged Rome to witness his canonization. In 1994, Bishop Javier Echeverría, above, became the third leader of Opus Dei. Below, the Pontifical University of the Holy Cross in Rome, where Opus Dei priests are trained.

The Exiles of Falun Gong

Repression drives a Chinese spiritual group into hiding

What does it take to become an outlaw in China? Promote democracy, organize an illicit labor union—or spend an early-morning hour in a park moving your hands around to form the shape of an imaginary wheel.

It was so easy to get pulled in, during those days in the late 1990s when Chinese society was still thawing out from decades of official repression. A friend might have mentioned that a new group was gathering in the local park to do a form of traditional Qi Gong exercises. One morning you found them, 20 or 30 people, under the yellow-and-red banner of Falun Gong—the Law of the Wheel Breathing Exercise—doing the slow-motion exercises to music from a tape recorder. There was no

fee, no formal teaching—they just invited you to join in and copy their movements.

It was gentle and somehow calming, and you went back the next morning. After several sessions, you were offered the book written by their "master," Li Hongzhi. It was about self-control and Buddhist enlightenment, written in a chatty style, and it cost only $2. The group would read and discuss parts of it after the exercises, so you bought a copy. The exercises got your circulation going, and meditation afterward helped dissipate frustrations from work and your crowded apartment block. China began to seem livable again.

Then came the big shock. What you didn't know was that you were being watched—that you and millions like

you were already caught in the net of China's biggest internal security operation since the Tiananmen Square crackdown in 1989. On July 22, 1999, the Chinese government announced that Falun Gong was banned—for practicing "evil thinking" and threatening social stability. All over China police began rounding up thousands of Falun Gong practitioners and driving them off to sports stadiums. There they were interrogated, sometimes for hours, and forced to sign letters disavowing the group. In scenes reminiscent of the nation's Cultural Revolution, more than 2 million books and instructional tapes were pulped or crushed by steam rollers in a single week. A nationwide system of collective guilt held police, factory bosses and family members accountable when people around them practiced Falun Gong.

The crackdown came after a secret three-month investigation of the sect by China's security services, during which agents infiltrated Falun Gong activities and clandestinely videotaped exercise sessions. The investigation was reportedly ordered by then President Jiang Zemin himself after a silent demonstration by 10,000 members of Falun Gong on April 25, 1999, outside Zhongnanhai, the Beijing compound where China's top leaders live. At that time the group said it was protesting magazine articles labeling it a superstitious cult, a charge that could have led to its being banned. Instead, its leaders said, it wanted to be recognized as a legitimate religious group.

The protest and subsequent clampdown introduced the world to a mystical movement little known outside Asia. Falun Gong is a variant of Qi Gong, a blend of mind and body work (it also includes Tai Chi) that strives to harness an energy called *Qi* (Chi). Qi Gong doesn't always rise to the intensity of faith, but charismatic "grand masters" have built up formidable followings on its principles. One such leader is Li Honghzi, who founded Falun Gong in 1992. The practice spread like wildfire through a restless China; by 1999, Beijing estimated that Falun Gong (also known as Falun Dafa) had 2 million adherents; the group claimed 100 million practitioners. Time estimated its size at 60 million—larger than China's Communist Party.

Ten years after Beijing outlawed Falun Gong, it is difficult to count the number of Falun Gong adherents, for they remain deeply sequestered, victims of official repression. The China Labour Bulletin, a Hong Kong–based human rights organization, estimated in 2007 that China's interior prison gulag holds more than 300,000 detainees, who are subject to "re-education through labor" for up to four years. Their inmates include members of Falun Gong as well as other religions banned by the state. A U.S. government watchdog group said that the regime tightened the screws of its "campaign of persecution" in 2008, as world attention focused on the Beijing Olympic Games.

The screws have not yet loosened. In 2009, Time reported the story of Beijing lawyer Li Chunfu, who in May went to the southwestern city of Chongqing with a colleague to meet with the family of a man who died in a labor camp. While meeting with the family, Li and lawyer Zhang Kai were detained by police. Li was chained to a chair and punched, while Zhang, also roughed up during the incident, was locked in a cage. Their transgression? They were representing the family of Jiang Xiqing, a man who belonged to the banned Falun Gong. ∎

Under fire *Above, Falun Gong members protest the banning of their movement in 1999 in Shanghai; the protests quickly subsided as China's regime cracked down.*

At right is Falun Gong founder Li Hongzhi in 1999, when he shared with Time *reporters his view that aliens have been visiting Earth since the early 1900s. In 2010 he remains in seclusion, at age 57*

法輪修煉大法
FALUN XIULIAN DAFA

Sins of the Fathers

Is a renegade Mormon cult practicing polygamy— or child abuse? And should the government step in?

As Jane Doe IV described her marriage in a Utah courtroom in 2007, spectators heard the details of what sounded like a terrible crime. She recalled on the witness stand the moment when her new husband began undressing her. She begged that he not touch her. "'I can't do this. Please don't,'" she remembered saying. "I was sobbing. My whole entire body was shaking, and I was so scared ... He just laid me onto the bed and had sex. It hurt," she said. "And I felt evil." Later, she went into the bathroom, swallowed the contents of a couple of bottles of over-the-counter pain pills and curled up on the floor. "I just wanted to die," she said.

The man she had married was her first cousin. And she was 14 years old.

What made this drama so confounding was that while this was a rape trial, the husband who allegedly assaulted Doe was a defense witness, not a defendant. And while the headlines called it a POLYGAMY TRIAL, that was not the charge either, though social attitudes about polygamy were clearly being put to the test. The defendant, Warren Jeffs, the prophet of the Fundamentalist Church of Jesus Christ of Latter Day Saints (FLDS), was being tried as an accomplice to rape for commanding Doe to agree to an arranged marriage, despite her resistance, and instructing her to submit to her husband "mind, body and soul" in order to be saved.

The FLDS was born more than a century ago when the Mormon church divided over the issue of plural marriage. Church founder Joseph Smith offered polygamy as one of the "eternal principles" of Mormonism, teaching that men would be exalted in heaven by marrying multiple wives on earth. In 1890, after years of penalties, persecution and seizure of church property, a new divine revelation inspired church leaders to reject the practice—which helped pave the way for Utah's statehood. But traditionalist Mormons thought the church was selling out and established their own fundamentalist sects, which continued the practice even as the larger church condemned it.

This was a case about what happens when the state's interest in protecting children runs up against a church's right to practice its beliefs, however repugnant others may find them. Jeffs' defense lawyers challenged the very notion that he should somehow be held responsible for what goes

Family matters
Above, an FLDS mother holds her child in April 2008, following the raid on the Yearning for Zion Ranch compound in Texas.

At right is FLDS elder Raymond Jessop during a recess in his Texas trial in October 2009, in which he was convicted of sexual abuse

on in the privacy of a marriage simply because he arranged it. To others, the issue was neither polygamy nor religion but simple sexual abuse. Utah state prosecutors had long looked for some way to penetrate the remote FLDS enclave headed by Jeffs, whose apostate refugees told stories of exploitation of children as workers, of incest and of sexual abuse. (He also led enclaves in Arizona and Texas.) But charges involving polygamy are notoriously hard to prove, especially in a sect so intent on making its own rules about what constitutes a marriage. So prosecutors shifted focus, turning to newly strengthened child-abuse and sexual-predator laws. Jeffs was tried and convicted on two counts of acting as an accomplice to rape.

Within months of Jeffs' Utah conviction, the focus on the FLDS shifted to Texas, where, on April 3, 2008, a convoy of state government vehicles converged on the Yearning for Zion Ranch, an Eldorado, Texas, compound that houses one of the largest FLDS groups in the U.S. Summoned by a call to a child-abuse hot line from a young girl who identified herself as "Sarah" and said that she and other minors were in danger, state officials removed 416 boys and girls from the ranch, more than anyone had realized were living there. The raid on the polygamist enclave produced haunting images: girls in calico dresses, removed from log cabin houses, looking questioningly into nowhere as they were led from their homes into a secular world they had been taught to fear. They sang hymns as they were driven away along with 139 adult women members of the sect.

The rest of the country was both appalled and fascinated, gawking at the sight of women seemingly dressed for *Little House on the Prairie,* whose modest appearance was jarringly at odds with their sexually aberrant lifestyle. First came the jokes, then some hard realities sank in. Hundreds of children were being separated from the only families they knew. Shuttled from one temporary facility to another, they were dispersed throughout Texas' over-taxed foster-care system, from the Panhandle to Houston. For weeks, investigators attempted to answer seemingly basic questions—like the identities of the children, many of whom gave different names and ages each time they were interviewed—and tried to unravel the complex maze of FLDS family relationships. While this frustrating work proceeded, no charges were filed, and the only public details of the alleged child abuse centered on several teen-age mothers found at the ranch, who were described in a request for a second search warrant.

By May, investigators came to the embarrassing conclusion that the call that triggered the raid was apparently a hoax: "Sarah" was actually an adult woman living in Colorado who had a history of impersonating victims of abuse. On May 29, the Texas Supreme Court ordered the state's child welfare authorities to return all the children to their parents.

In 2009 Texas authorities were vindicated in part when FLDS elder Raymond Jessop, 38, was convicted of sexual assault on an underage girl—said to be one of his nine wives—in a case arising from evidence gathered in the 2008 raid. As emboldened authorities began scrutinizing FLDS practices more closely, the story moved north: on Jan. 7, 2009, British Columbia Attorney General Wally Oppal ordered the arrest on polygamy charges of Winston Blackmore, then 52, and James Oler, 44, the leaders of an FLDS settlement called Bountiful in the small town of Lister, B.C. According to press accounts, Blackmore is alleged to have as many as 26 wives and 108 children. ∎

Prophet, Fugitive, Prisoner

When FLDS prophet Rulon Jeffs died in 2002, his son Warren took over his position, though sect leadership had not been inherited previously. Warren, 54 in 2010, also inherited many of his father's 75 wives and established himself as more strict and separatist than his father. He outlawed basketball games and holidays and inveighed against newspapers, TV and the Internet (though he distributed his speeches to followers via iPods).

In 2005 Jeffs was indicted for sex crimes in Arizona and Utah and became a fugitive; he was arrested in August 2006 in Las Vegas, while on the FBI's 10-most-wanted list. He was convicted in Utah in September 2007, left, and in January 2010 he was serving five years to life in an Arizona prison, as he awaited a new trial on charges of sexual assault and bigamy in that state.

A wholesome life? *On the surface, FLDS life can seem charmingly innocent, evoking bygone ways. Above, Teresa Jeffs, 16, daughter of FLDS prophet Warren Jeffs, goes airborne in New Braunfels, Texas. But evidence gathered during the 2008 raid on the Yearning for Zion Ranch included two photos of young girls—one age 12, the other 13—sitting in Jeffs' lap and embracing him and kissing him. One picture was marked "first anniversary," and the other was marked as a wedding photo*

Simple pleasures *Helaman Jeffs, 16, yawns as four sons and a son-in-law of Warren Jeffs prepare to sing hymns in New Braunfels, Texas. Under Jeffs, sons and daughters of FLDS members were kept strictly separated until church elders decreed they were ready to be married. On the mantel are photographs of FLDS patriarch Jeffs, left, and his father Rulon*

"Do What Thou Wilt" *Faces of the occult: at left, a carefully coiffed female disciple of Crowley's shows her tattooed "Mark of the Beast"; at center, Crowley in power headgear; at right, Golden Dawn co-founder Samuel Mathers in full regalia*

Adventures in the Occult
The Order of the Golden Dawn explored alternate knowledge

Magic is the earliest of man's religious responses. Anthropologists suspect that the first known sculpture of a human being—the "Venus of Hohle Fels," a carving of a voluptuous female discovered in Germany in 2008 and dated to 35,000 B.C.—was created to honor and ensure fertility. The primitive but striking animal paintings in the caves of early humans are sympathetic magic, an attempt to guarantee success in the hunt. Online horoscopes are a direct legacy from the astronomer priests of Babylonia—the same magicians, or Magi, who are said to have seen Christ's birth foretold in the heavens. Even as Christianity spread through Europe, for centuries magical arts and the new creed lived in uneasy coexistence. The fascination of millions with magic, astronomy and occult knowledge has never gone away; every decade or two it simply dons new clothes to adapt to, uh, a New Age.

In the early 20th century, mystical inquiry wore the robes of the group that styled itself the Hermetic Order of the Golden Dawn. This most famous of occult secret societies was founded in the late 19th century by three British Freemasons: William Westcott, William Woodman and Samuel Mathers. But its leadership was soon hijacked by a man who reveled in his reputation as "the wickedest man in the world," Aleister Crowley (1875-1947), the Marilyn Manson of the Edwardian age.

How wicked was this wicked man? Well, he claimed to have seduced a kitchen maid at 14 while his mother was at church, and to have butchered a cat to see whether it had nine lives. His mother called him "the Beast"; he one-upped her by styling himself "The Beast Whose Number is 666." He spent his inherited fortune pursuing his creed, which he dubbed Thelema, and whose first law is, "There is no law beyond Do What Thou Wilt."

What Crowley wilt was to attract young men and women with his mystical ramblings, write pornographic poems and explore automatic writing, inscribing the thoughts of spirit beings—a.k.a. "the Secret Chiefs"—while under the influence of opium, hashish and pharmaceuticals. British newspapers feasted on fantastic stories of his doings: he could raise devils and dead cats; he drank blood; he celebrated the obscene Black Mass with naked nymphs in the "temple" he set up in his London flat. It was a busy life, yet even its many delights faded over time: "I want blasphemy, murder, rape, revolution, anything, bad or good, but strong," he declared in later years.

Crowley's quest for strength led him to satanism, animal sacrifice, "sex magick" and heroin addiction. Before his death in 1947, he lent his fame to an occult secret society called the Order of the Oriental Templars. The group still operates a small number of lodges around the world, where believers continue to pursue the path first explored by Crowley. Spoiler alert: That path may be wicked. ∎

Modern magus
In the undated, damaged photograph above, Crowley is shown conducting occult rites, probably in his London flat on Chancery Lane or at his estate on Loch Ness in Scotland

The Cult Mentality

Manson Family Values

With psychedelics and psychobabble, a charismatic guru created a cult for the countercultural era

We were riding on the wind," the enthusiastic young woman assured jurors in a California courtroom in 1971, as she related tales of her life in a communal group of hippies led by a charismatic would-be musician. The man she vouched for at a sentencing trial resembled a modern-day saint. "Charlie is a man," testified Lynette Alice Fromme, 22, "and we were all looking for a man who would be at our feet in his love but would not let us step on him. Charlie was a father who knew that it is good to make love, and makes love with love, but not with evil and guilt."

Describing the radically unordered lifestyle of the extended artificial "Family" that surrounded leader Charles Manson, Fromme declared, "You could say it's a nonsense world of *Alice in Wonderland,* but it makes a lot of sense. Everybody makes their own rules ... Each moment is different."

Fromme, who was christened "Squeaky" within the Manson Family, isn't the only young American to have tasted the tie-dyed allure of the hippie lifestyle in the 1960s— but she is among those who helped bring the soaring, innocent dreams of the Age of Aquarius crashing to the ground. For the 35-year-old man she came to think of as her father was no ordinary counterculture guru: he was a psychopath who appropriated the peace-'n'-love vibe of the times to create a cult of followers so dazed and confused that they were prepared to follow his every command—even when that command was the murder of innocent people.

On Aug. 9, 1969, four of Manson's black-clad followers murdered pregnant actress Sharon Tate, wife of film director Roman Polanski, and four visitors to her Los Angeles estate. The murders were gruesome in the extreme, involving numerous stabbings and shootings; the word PIG was written on the kitchen door in Tate's blood. The next night, Family members brutally murdered a married couple, Leno and Rosemary LaBianca, in their Los Angeles home, again leaving three messages, including HEALTER SKELTER [sic], written in blood.

Manson, who ordered the murders, was not present during the killings. Nor, incredibly, did he know any of the people he sentenced to death. The Tate victims apparently died because Manson, an aspiring songwriter, nursed a grudge against actress Doris Day's record-producer son, Terry Melcher,

Charlie's children
Blissed-out Family members, top right, gather at Manson's 1970 trial; Lynette "Squeaky" Fromme, on far left, did not take part in the 1969 murders but tried to assassinate President Gerald Ford in 1975.
At right, Manson enters the courtroom during his trial, while cult member Susan Atkins eyes the camera. She died in a California prison on Sept. 24, 2009.
At top, a 2009 prison mug shot of Manson at 74

RIGHT: ASSOCIATED PRESS (2); LEFT: POLARIS

Hideout *Manson first began forming his Family in San Francisco in 1967, but he moved the group to the Los Angeles area in 1968. The Family ended up living on the Spahn Ranch outside the city, above, rent free— after Manson assigned female followers to supply sexual favors to its elderly owner*

who had refused to record one of Manson's songs. Tate had rented the Melcher house, grounds for a death sentence in Manson's world. The LaBiancas, who owned a grocery business, were picked at random from the ranks of the city's affluent. Somewhere behind these all-too-real horrors was Manson's all-too-fanciful delusion that a string of senseless killings would create a racial apocalypse in Los Angeles, a goal he apparently considered desirable, given that he was engaged in a dispute with a black drug dealer over a deal gone wrong. He called this bizarre scenario "Helter Skelter," a term he lifted from a song on the Beatles' eponymous "white album," released late in 1968.

The search for the killers was bungled by Los Angeles police, but some three months after the August murders, Manson and the members of his gang were finally apprehended, thanks to the jailhouse chatter of a Family member held on a different charge. The trial took an unprecedented nine months, hypnotizing the nation. The determined prosecutor, Vincent Bugliosi, won death sentences for Manson and his killers. (California later temporarily struck down the death penalty, and the sentences were commuted to life.)

Bugliosi's firsthand account of the case, *Helter Skelter,* published in 1974, remains a primary source for students of the events.

Forty years after the dreadful murders, the questions linger: How are psychopaths like Manson formed, and how do they succeed in exerting such mesmerizing sway over their followers as to turn them into remote-controlled assassins? Manson's life story, sadly, is of a kind familiar to police, prosecutors and psychologists. Born in 1934 to a teenage mother, he never saw his father. His prostitute parent was often in jail, and young Manson was shifted around from relatives to foster parents to reformatories. As he grew up, he turned to petty crime, mainly car theft. His education stopped at the seventh grade. When he was arrested, TIME called him "a drifter with a five-page criminal record stretching back 20 years."

Maybe so. But Manson was also a drifter with the gift of gab, an arresting gaze and a way with young women. And he found an ally in the times in which he lived: while he used many of the standard tactics of a cult leader, he also exploited the restless energies of the 1960s to attract and control his flock.

In and out of prison, Manson became interested in music and the occult, and when he was last released, in 1967, he headed for San Francisco as a "roving minstrel." Perfect timing. In the Summer of Love, the streets of the city were filled with young people who had left mainstream society behind—or whose parents, like Fromme's, had turned them out of the house. Enter surrogate father figure Charles Manson.

As the Family grew and Manson's grip tightened, he isolated the group, creating the us-vs.-them stance with normal society that is fundamental to the cult mind. He moved the Family to Los Angeles, settling in at an old dude ranch used as a set for western films. And he rechristened his followers, giving them names that signalled their new allegiance to him: Fromme became "Squeaky," and Susan Atkins, 21, became "Sadie Mae Glutz." When "Sadie" had a son, Manson named him Zezozose Zadfrack Glutz.

Mini-Mes *When Manson shaved his head during his murder trial, his zombie-like female followers, seen above camped outside the courtroom, followed suit*

Such practices are standard issue in cult life. But Manson also appropriated the mores of the '60s to shape his disciples. He assumed control of their sex lives, leading group orgies and demanding the favors of his young female followers, whom he encouraged to loll harem-like around the commune nude or barebreasted. He kept on the good side of the octogenarian ranch owner, George Spahn, by assigning his "girls" to flirt and play sexual games with him.

Drugs were another powerful tool in Manson's arsenal; he freely passed out LSD and marijuana, further addling the brains of his followers. And his command of mystical mumbo-jumbo kept his flock in awe. At times he claimed he was the reincarnation of Christ: after all, his name signified he was the Son of Man. Dazzled Family members called him both "God" and "Satan."

Over time, Manson's megalomania turned into full-blown paranoia, and he began ordering his minions to dress in black outfits and sneak into homes in exclusive neighborhoods of L.A. He called these sophomoric excursions "creepy-crawl" missions, and they enhanced his followers' notion that they were rebels engaged in the noble adventure of subverting a misguided society of "pigs."

When the allure of these jaunts began to pale, Manson upped the ante: now the stakes were death. "That man has wronged me," he said, referring to Melcher, who no longer lived in the home now occupied by Tate. "Society has wronged me. We'll kill whatever pigs are in that house. Go in there and get them." The tragedy is not that he ordered the senseless murders but that his morally bewildered followers obeyed them.

In 2009, as the 40th anniversary of the murders was observed, TIME interviewed Bugliosi. When asked if he regarded Manson as mentally ill or purely evil, his prosecutor replied, "His moral values were completely twisted and warped, but let's not confuse that with insanity. He was crazy in the way that Hitler was crazy. In fact, Hitler was Manson's greatest hero—he spoke about Hitler all the time. He said that Hitler had the right answer for everything, that he was a tuned-in guy. So he's not crazy—he's an evil, sophisticated con man. We're talking about evil here, as opposed to mental illness. Manson wanted to kill as many people as he could." He will kill no more: as of 2010, Manson, now 75, remains incarcerated at Corcoran State Prison near Fresno, Calif. ∎

Led to the Slaughter

Cult leader Jim Jones instigates a mass suicide

The large central building was ringed by bright colors. It looked like a parking lot filled with cars. When the plane dipped lower, the cars turned out to be bodies. Scores and scores of bodies—hundreds of bodies—wearing red dresses, blue T shirts, green blouses, pink slacks, children's polka-dotted jumpers. Couples with their arms around each other, children holding parents. Nothing moved. Washing hung on the clotheslines. The fields were freshly plowed. Banana trees and grape vines were flourishing. But nothing moved."

So reported TIME Correspondent Donald Neff, one of the first newsmen to fly into the hitherto obscure hamlet of Jonestown in the jungles of Guyana, on the northern coast of South America, in late November 1978. The scene below him was one of almost unimaginable carnage. In an appalling demonstration of the way in which a charismatic leader can bend the minds of his followers with a devilish blend of professed altruism and psychological tyranny, some 900 members of the California-based Peoples Temple died in a self-imposed ritual of mass suicide and murder.

The followers of the Rev. Jim Jones, 47, a once respected Indiana-born humanitarian who degenerated into egomania and paranoia, had first ambushed a party of visiting Americans, killing California Congressman Leo Ryan, 53, three journalists and one defector from their heavily guarded colony at Jonestown. Then, exhorted by their leader, intimidated by armed guards and lulled with

sedatives, parents and nurses used syringes to squirt a concoction of potassium cyanide and potassium chloride onto the tongues of babies. The adults and older children picked up paper cups and sipped the same deadly poison sweetened by purple Flavor Aid.

Ryan began inquiring about Jim Jones and his followers, who had just started clearing some 900 acres in the rain forests of Guyana, after unhappy relatives of Temple members, as well as a few people who had fearfully left the cult, told the Congressman that beatings and blackmail, rather than brotherly love, impelled the cultists to work on the new colony. Articles in *New West* magazine and the San Francisco *Examiner* in August 1977 further documented the Temple's increasing use of violence to enforce conformity to its rigid rules of conduct. Members were routinely scolded by Jones before the assembled community and then whipped or beaten with paddles for such infractions as smoking or failing to pay attention during a Jones "sermon." A woman accused of having a romance with a male cult member was forced to have intercourse with a man she disliked, while the entire colony watched. One means of indoctrinating children: electrodes were attached to their arms and legs, and they were told to smile at the mention of their leader's name. Everyone was ordered to call Jones "Father."

The endgame at Jonestown began with the arrival of Congressman Ryan, who represented a district in Northern California where relatives of some of the cult members lived. Ryan, urged by a group of concerned relatives of Peoples Temple members, traveled

False prophet
Above, Jones at the height of his sway over his followers. From early on, part of his appeal was his embrace of all races in his flock, and members of his Peoples Temple spent many hours in community service. But Jones increasingly showed the signs of apocalyptic megalomania; in Guyana, he began speaking of the need for "revolutionary suicide."

At right, the ghastly scene in Jonestown after the mass suicide, with a metal vat that held the poison drink in the foreground

Murder at the airstrip *Bodies lie on the ground at the Port Kaituma airport, where Peoples Temple members killed five people and injured 11. This picture was taken by reporter Tim Reiterman with the camera of slain photographer Greg Robinson. Reiterman's recollections of the events are at right*

to Guyana with government officials, nine journalists and members of the relatives' group.

The visitors arrived in a chartered aircraft, an 18-seat De Havilland Otter, at an airstrip in Port Kaituma, six miles from Jonestown. They rode to the colony along a muddy and barely passable road through the jungle in a tractor-drawn flat-bed trailer. At Jonestown all were greeted warmly by a smiling Jones.

The Temple members put on a marvelous performance for their visitors. Reporters were led past the central, open-air pavilion, used as both a school and an assembly hall. They saw the newly completed sawmill, the 10,000-volume library, the neat nursery. An evening of entertainment in the pavilion followed. As a band beat out a variety of tunes, the colonists burst into song, including a rousing chorus of *America the Beautiful.* Even the skeptical Ryan was impressed. But the next day, the reality of Jones' sway over his followers was made clear. A few Temple members approached the visiting delegation, saying they were desperate to leave Jonestown. As Ryan conferred with Jones about their request, he was attacked with a knife by cult member Don Sly but wasn't harmed. As Sly was subdued, Jones watched impassively. He made no move to interfere.

Congressman Ryan appeared calm as his group prepared to depart. The party again headed down the rutted road to the Port Kaituma airport. Several Jones loyalists trailed the delegation back to the airstrip and opened fire. Ryan and four other members of the group were killed. Eleven people were injured.

Those who survived fled into the jungle, where some of the fugitive Temple members spoke of the "white night" exercises in which loudspeakers would summon all Jonestown residents from sleep to convene in the central pavilion, where Jones would harangue them about "the beauty of dying." All would line up and be given a drink described as poison. They would take it, expecting to die. Then Jones would tell them the liquid was not poisonous; they had passed his "loyalty test."

The survivors had no way of knowing that Jones had already ordered the ultimate white night to begin back in the Jonestown commune, as soon as he heard of Ryan's death. One of the few survivors of the events, Odell Rhodes, told TIME that many mothers voluntarily gave the cyanide to their children, then swallowed the poison themselves. Seated on the high wicker chair that served as his throne, Jones kept urging the crowd on. Said Rhodes: "Babies were screaming, children were screaming, and there was mass confusion."

Nevertheless, the lethal drinking continued. Cultists filled their cups from a metal vat on a table at the center of the pavilion, then wandered off to die, often in family groups, their arms wrapped lovingly around one another. The tranquilizers in the liquid may have dulled their senses; it took about five minutes for them to die. In the end, some 900 people followed Jones into death, although Jones apparently never drank the poison. He was found near his throne dead of a gunshot wound. The bullet was fired at close range, either by Jones or a close aide. ∎

A Reporter Looks Back, 30 Years Later

Witnesses *Tim Reiterman, at right, takes notes in Georgetown, Guyana, en route to Jonestown. At center is reporter Ron Javers, who also survived. At left is another survivor, Carol Boyd, who was related to two Temple members*

No one knows more about the Jonestown massacre than journalist Tim Reiterman. He began investigating the Rev. Jim Jones and his cult for the San Francisco *Examiner* 18 months before Jones burst on the world's stage some 30 years ago. Reiterman was one of the journalists who accompanied Congressman Leo Ryan to Jonestown, Guyana. On Nov. 18, 1978, after meeting with Jones and his followers, their small party was ambushed by Peoples Temple gunmen at the local airport. Ryan and four others were killed; Reiterman himself was wounded.

After recovering from his injuries, Reiterman spent the next four years researching and writing a comprehensive book about the tragedy, *Raven: The Untold Story of the Rev. Jim Jones and His People* (reissued in 2008 by Tarcher/Penguin). The 624-page book is an extraordinary act of scholarship, the definitive account of an event that continues to fascinate and mystify. TIME senior reporter Andrea Sachs spoke to Reiterman about his experiences in 2008, the 30th anniversary of the events.

TIME: Was Jim Jones a bad person from the beginning, or did he grow into one?
Tim Reiterman: Good and evil coexisted in Jim Jones throughout his life. I really do believe ... that the seeds of [his] madness were there from his earliest years. He was somewhat neglected as a child. He was part of an unconventional family where his mother was the bread-winner and his father was a brooding man ... Jones sought out acceptance and a sense of family through churches, but at the same time he had a tremendous need for power and control. He would conduct little church services up in the loft of a barn and lock his playmates in there; later he used a firearm to try to control his best friend. These early incidents, as well as some cruelty to animals, were harbingers for the sickness that grew in him over the years.

What was your impression of Jones when you interviewed him in Guyana?
He did not appear to be well. His skin appeared sallow. His eyes were almost gelatinous. His handshake seemed rather weak, and when he spoke there was a constant undercurrent of paranoia. He was clearly viewing himself as a martyr and it was very bothersome to realize that over 900 lives were in the hands of this man.

When you and the Congressman's group got ready to leave Jonestown, what happened?
Fifteen people stepped forward [asking to leave] ... and both of these families were long-time followers of Jim Jones ... The mood of Jonestown grew darker as this day went on, and late in the afternoon the clouds turned black and there was this freakish wind that just tore through the pavilion as I was talking with Jones. Then there was this torrent of rain. He basically said that the Temple was being destroyed from within, and what he meant by that was that these defectors were going to tell the world eventually what was really going on inside Jonestown, and that the end was drawing near. So it was a very ominous moment before we even left Jonestown.

What happened when you went to your plane?
During that boarding procedure, a Temple tractor-drawn trailer full of gunmen raced toward us. They jumped out and they started firing. That's when I was hit by gunfire as I was trying to take cover behind one of the plane wheels. Fortunately I was only hit in the arm a couple of times and was able to jump up and sprint to the jungle and take cover.

Do you think that the 900 deaths that immediately followed were suicides, or were they murders?
I believe that this was a mass murder. First of all, there were over 200 children who could not have formed the intent to commit suicide. Second, Jim Jones had isolated his people and conditioned them through suicide rehearsals and mock sieges to accept death. Third, he orchestrated the events on that final day so that the outcome was never in doubt. He had gunmen go shoot the Congressman. Then he turned around to his followers, once he got news the Congressman was dead, and announced it. He said, Now some among us have done something that's going to cause the army to come in here and nobody will be safe. Let's bring forward the potion and let's bring the children first. By having the children die first, he sealed the fate of their parents and other elders, because no one would have any reason to live.

Apocalypse Now

A psychopath leads his followers into a longed-for inferno

There were occasions when David Koresh enforced discipline among his followers at their walled compound outside Waco, Texas, the hard way. One of his hand-picked lieutenants would paddle the rule breakers with an oar on which were inscribed the words IT IS WRITTEN. Most of the time that wasn't necessary. In the manner of cult leaders before him, Koresh held sway largely through means that were both more subtle and more degrading. Food was rationed in unpredictable ways. Newcomers were gradually relieved of their bank accounts and personal possessions. And while the men were subjected to an uneasy celibacy, Koresh took their wives and daughters as his concubines.

All of it just confirmed his power in the eyes of his personal flock of Branch Davidians, an apocalyptic Christian sect that traces its roots to divisions within the fundamentalist Seventh-Day Adventist Church in the 1920 and '30s. And for anyone who thought it odd that a holy man lived out a teenage boy's sexual fantasy, Koresh had a mangled theological rationale. He was Jesus Christ in sinful form, who because he indulged the flesh could judge mankind with insights that the first, more virtuous Messiah had lacked. Or as he put it in one of his harangues: "Now what better sinner can know a sinner than a godly sinner? Huh?"

Equipped with both a creamy charm and a cold-blooded willingness to manipulate those drawn to him, Koresh was a type well known to students of cult practices: the charismatic leader with a pathological edge, like Charles Manson and Jim Jones. Like Jones, Koresh fashioned a tight-knit community that saw itself at desperate odds with the world outside. He plucked

sexual partners as he pleased from among his followers and formed an élite guard of lieutenants to enforce his will. And like Jones, he led his disciples to their doom: Koresh, 50 other adults and 25 children under 15 died on April 19, 1993, in their flaming compound during a Federal Government raid that followed a long siege by authorities—and that remains highly controversial.

Psychologists are inclined to classify Koresh as a psychopath, always with the reminder that such people can be nothing short of enchanting on a first encounter. "The psychopath is often charming, bright, very persuasive. He quickly wins people's trust and is uncannily adept at manipulating and conning people," Louis West, a professor of psychiatry at the University of California at Los Angeles medical school, told TIME after the deadly raid.

David Koresh was born Vernon Wayne Howell in 1959 to an unwed mother; he never met his father. He dropped out of his Texas high school in his first year and joined the Branch Davidian movement in 1981; by the late 1980s he was the head of his own sect; he moved his followers to a compound called Mount Carmel about 10 miles outside Waco and renamed it Ranch Apocalypse. Once in the cult, Davidians surrendered all material means of personal independence, like money and belongings, while Koresh seemed to have unlimited funds, much of the money apparently from his followers' nest eggs. Koresh drove a black Camaro muscle car, but his faithful kept their woeful clunkers running by cannibalizing for spare parts the old automobiles that littered the grounds of the compound.

At lengthy sessions of biblical preaching that cult

members attended twice a day, Koresh underlined his authority by impressing upon them that he alone understood the Scriptures. He changed his interpretations at will, while his unsteady flock struggled to keep up. In a tactic common to cult leaders, Koresh made food a tool for ensuring obedience. The compound diet was often insufficient, varying according to the leader's whim. Sometimes dinner was stew or chicken; at other times it might be nothing but popcorn. On their infrequent trips to Waco, cultists could be seen wolfing down packaged cheese in convenience stores.

Having convinced followers that he was the Messiah, Koresh went on to convince them that because his seed was divine, only he had the right to procreate. Even as Koresh bedded their wives and daughters—some as young as 11—in his comfortable private bedroom on the second floor of the ranch house, the men were confined to their dormitory downstairs. Behind the mind games and psychological sadism lay the threat of physical force. In addition to the paddlings, offenders could be forced down into a pit of raw sewage, then not allowed to clean up.

As the Davidians stockpiled guns and ammunition, Koresh's theology centered more obsessively upon the coming Apocalypse, binding both Koresh and his followers in a vision of shared catastrophe in order to maintain their focus and resist the overtures of the authorities. "Koresh would say we would have to suffer, that we were going to be persecuted and some of us would be killed and tortured," David Bunds recalled. He left the group in 1989—four years before its fiery demise.

As Koresh heightened the melodrama, the cult's ties with the outside world became irretrievably broken. "The adulation of this confined group works on this charismatic leader so that he in turn spirals into greater and greater paranoia," Murray Miron, a psychologist who advised the FBI during the standoff, told TIME. "He's playing a role that his followers have cast him in." In the end, Koresh and his flock may have magnified one another's needs. He looked to them to confirm his belief that he was God's appointed one, destined for a martyr's death. They looked to him to bring their spiritual wanderings to a close. In the flames of Ranch Apocalypse, sadly, they all may have found what they were searching for. ∎

Death, as foretold

Controversy lingers over the raid on Koresh's compound outside Waco in April 1993 by federal agencies under FBI control. Critics charge the raid, which followed a 51-day standoff, was ill timed and the deaths could have been avoided.

In the days before the raid, Koresh sent the FBI two "letters from God," penned on lavender notepaper by one of his 19 wives. "I AM your God," he said in one, "and you will bow under my feet. Do you think you have the power to stop my will?" At left, Koresh in 1989

The Chosen Few

What distinguishes a cult from a religion? Submission of one's will to a strong leader or the group; a paranoid stance against mainstream society; self-denial, strict regimentation and the erasure of one's old identity. Above all, point of view—for one man's religion is another man's cult

LEFT: BROOKS KRAFT—SYGMA/CORBIS. RIGHT, CLOCKWISE FROM TOP LEFT: PAUL HANNA—REUTERS/LANDOV; AHN YOUNG-JOON—ASSOCIATED PRESS; BETTMANN/CORBIS; ROBIN DONINA SERNE—ST. PETERSBURG TIMES/ZUMA

Heaven's Gate

In a spacious mansion in Rancho Santa Fe, Calif., 39 bodies were laid out on their backs on bunk beds and mattresses, looking like so many laboratory specimens pinned neatly to a board. Each was dressed in black pants, flowing black shirt, spanking-new black Nikes. Their faces were hidden by purple cloths, the color of Christian penance. All, helpfully, bore identification papers for the authorities to find.

In performing their group suicide in March, 1997, the 39 members of the Heaven's Gate cult expressed their longtime conviction that their bodies were merely irrelevant "containers," to be left behind when they were whisked away by extraterrestrials. To show their disdain for bodily pleasures, seven of the dead men, including leader Marshall Applewhite, above, had had themselves castrated before their deaths.

The UFO cult was founded by Applewhite and Bonnie Nettles, who called themselves Do and Ti or Bo and Peep; she died in 1985. They plucked bits and pieces of various doctrines like birds building a nest, intertwining New Age symbols, science-fiction motifs and ancient religions. In a final housekeeping detail, the cultists left behind videotape press kits explaining their mass suicide as essential to beginning a new life.

Scientology

It calls itself the Church of Scientology, and its 8 million members around the world sternly insist they belong to a religion rather than a cult. But in 2008, when investigating magistrate Jean-Christophe Hullin filed the findings of a nine-year inquiry in France in which he charged six of the group's leaders in that nation with intentional fraud, he described Scientology as "first and foremost a commercial business" whose interactions with followers are defined by "a real obsession for financial remuneration."

Scientology was founded by sci-fi writer L. Ron Hubbard in the 1950s. Its most prominent spokesman is actor Tom Cruise, shown at top speaking at a Scientology event in Spain. In a 2009 series of articles in the St. Petersburg *Times,* former insiders described current leader David Miscavige, inset, as a brutal tyrant who was violently abusive on multiple occasions to his lieutenants.

Unification Church

On Oct. 14, 2009, the Rev. Sun Myung Moon conducted one of the events that have become the signature of his Unification Church: a mass wedding in which he married some 40,000 people at once in locations around the world. Thirty-three years before, in 1976, TIME observed, "Although Sun Myung Moon sometimes appears to be a Christian evangelist, he is in actuality the megalomaniacal 'messiah' of a new religion." Maybe so, but Moon and church have prospered over the course of those decades: as of 2010, the church has some few hundred thousand members, many of whom claim to believe their Korean-born leader, now 90, is the living reincarnation of Jesus Christ. Moon spreads his strongly conservative political views through the Washington *Times,* the newspaper he founded in 1982. The picture below shows a mass wedding in South Korea in 2005.

Bhagwan Shree Rajneesh

At its height in the early 1980s, the incorporated city of Rajneeshpuram in Oregon's Wasco County was a sight to behold. Its leader, the Bhagwan, one of a lengthy string of Indian holy men who have taken their teachings to the West with great success, toured his 64,000-acre ranch with armed guards in one of his 90 Rolls-Royces. His 1,300 followers, mostly middle-class refugees from urban living, dressed in bright colors and grooved on the guru's celebration of the spiritual power of sexuality.

The community collapsed in 1985, after federal authorities filed charges against the Bhagwan of violating immigration laws; he had also fallen out with his closest followers amid allegations of murder threats and attempted poisonings. The Bhagwan was deported late in 1985 and returned to India, where he died in 1990, age 58.

Outside the Law

Death of a Don *The body of New York City Mafia leader Paul Castellano lies on the street following his murder outside a Manhattan steakhouse on Dec. 16, 1985. John Gotti Sr., who succeeded Castellano as head of the city's Gambino crime family, was convicted in 1992 of ordering the hit*

When Hatred Wears a Hood

The Ku Klux Klan, fueled by the poison of fear and racism, is America's most notorious secret society

The burning cross. The white, pointed hoods. The midnight raids. The merciless lynchings and grisly murders. The code of silence, the secret rites of initiation, the cosy complicity of police and judges: over a period of some 145 years, the hallmarks of America's most notorious secret society, the Ku Klux Klan, have branded themselves on the national psyche. Nourished by grievance and misplaced pride, the Klan flourishes whenever racial hatred and fear peak—in the wake of the Civil War, as waves of immigrants transformed America's face, as blacks began to win full civil rights and as an African-American man was sworn in as President of the U.S. For as of 2010, the Ku Klux Klan is still not a subject for the history books: it is the stuff of headlines.

This most infamous of secret societies started as something of a lark, an amusement for Civil War veterans with time on their hands and grudges to nurse. In the winter of 1865-66 in Pulaski, Tenn., six young ex-Confederate officers got together to form a club. Like college kids, they gave their group all the trappings of a fraternity—mysterious rites, initiations, secret words. For a name, they hit on the Greek word for circle, *kyklos,* gave it a few twists and came up with Ku

Klux Klan. For kicks, they made robes and hoods out of bedsheets and pillow cases, and took to riding sheet-draped horses solemnly through the town at night. Soon they discovered that their frolics frightened superstitious blacks, and that was reason enough for scores of other young white men to join in the "fun," which quickly turned all too serious, as horseplay gave way to racial intimidation.

Klansmen soon organized nationally, the better to fight the hated Reconstruction agenda of Northern politicians. In Nashville, in 1867, they drew up a constitution, named Confederate General Nathan Bedford Forrest their Imperial Wizard and turned to terrorism. Hidden in their sheets and masks, they rode the countryside thirsting for violence. Anyone—white or black—who cooperated with Reconstruction was fair game for barbarism. White men who taught in African-American schools were lashed, and the schools were set afire and reduced to ashes. Blacks who refused to work for white men, or who flourished on their own, were thrashed with whips; some were hanged, some castrated, some burned to death, some murdered and quartered like animals.

For the most part, the Klan's outrages were applauded by Southerners who felt that the K.K.K. was the last best hope for the re-

The religion of racism *At right, spectators gather around a burning cross in Livingston Parish, La., in 1975. Hoods maintained the anonymity of Klan members, but the event was advertised in local publications.*

Above, Klan members in police custody in Mississippi in 1879

gion's lily-white cause. In 1869, Forrest ordered the Klan to disband; it did not. With the end of Reconstruction after the 1876 presidential election, the K.K.K. lost its most powerful reason for existence. But through the end of the 19th century, Klansmen helped enforce the unwritten codes of the Jim Crow era, keeping African Americans "in their place"—separate and distinctly unequal.

The Klan mentality never died; it merely lay quiescent, while apologists fed it intravenously with myths. Thomas Dixon Jr.'s 1905 book, *The Clansman,* idealized the K.K.K. as righteous crusaders led by noble men. After D.W. Griffith immortalized the Klan in his 1915 film of Dixon's book, *The Birth of a Nation,* the group enjoyed a national renascence, this time as a populist political force whose equal-opportunity hatred was directed at any American not born a white Protestant of northern European descent.

On Thanksgiving eve 1915, itinerant Methodist preacher William Joseph Simmons took 15 friends to the top of Stone Mountain, near Atlanta; built an altar on which he placed a U.S. flag, a Bible and an unsheathed sword; set fire to a crude wooden cross; muttered incantations about a "practical fraternity among men"; and declared himself Imperial Wizard of the Invisible Empire of the Knights of the Ku Klux Klan.

Under Simmons, the Klan drifted along for four years with a few thousand members. Then Simmons hired Edward Young Clarke, a press agent and gifted fund raiser. He set forth the Klan's goal in terms of Christian morality vs. sin. The enemies of America, the new-model Klan proclaimed, were booze, loose women, Jews, blacks and Roman Catholics (whose "dago" Pope was bent on taking over the U.S.). Across the nation, as clergymen lent the K.K.K. massive support, it blossomed into a mighty organization that claimed about 4 million members in its hooded ranks. The Klan played a major role in the 1924 and 1928 presidential campaigns and helped elect other officeholders, from judges and mayors to Senators and Congressmen.

Behind the scenes, Klansmen now resumed their reign of terror as self-appointed judges, juries and executioners. They tarred and feathered men and women—white and black—whom they suspected of illicit sexual relations, and lynched, mutilated or lashed hundreds of others. The Klan's operations provided tidy profits for its leaders in donations and merchandise sales, but by the late 1920s the resurgence was ebbing. Several states invoked anti-Klan laws; others forbade the Klan to wear masks. Corruption and internecine battles for leadership further weakened the organization. In the 1930s a diminished Klan cuddled up to U.S. Nazis and

Chronicles of The Klan

Founded in fun, the Ku Klux Klan evolved into a violent secret militia that fought Reconstruction and integration in the South. Its influence has waxed and waned—but never disappeared—in the 145 years since the group was created in Tennessee by six former Confederate soldiers in 1865-66

1867
Former Confederate General Nathan Bedford Forrest was chosen to lead the Klan in 1867, soon after its founding. As the vanquished South felt the full weight of Reconstruction descend, the Klan offered an anonymous means of intimidating newly empowered blacks. Forrest may have regretted his Klan affiliation; he ordered the group to disband in 1869—without success.

1871
John Campbell, a freed black, vainly begs for mercy from Ku Klux Klansmen in Moore County, N.C., in August 1871, as depicted in a contemporary wood engraving. Note the horned hoods, a style favored by early Klansmen but later put aside. The U.S. government passed four Force Acts in the early 1870s that helped subdue the early Klan's reign of terror.

1915

Kentucky-born film director D.W. Griffith helped lead the Klan's resurgence in the early 20th century with his glorified portrayal of the group in his epic set in the Reconstruction era, *The Birth of a Nation.* The silent film, featuring a host of technical innovations that advanced the art of cinema, became a blockbuster that spurred interest in the Klan. Two decades later, another epic tale of the South, Margaret Mitchell's *Gone With the Wind,* also portrayed slaveholders as sympathetic paternalists and depicted those who fought against full rights for African Americans as heroes, supporting the Klan's cause.

1920s

At left, Klansmen parade through the streets of Red Bank, N.J., in 1925, during the Klan's second heyday. In the '20s, members of a resurgent Klan tortured Jewish shopkeepers, whom they accused of massive international financial conspiracies, and they published a spurious Knights of Columbus "oath" that portrayed Roman Catholics as villainous conspirators against the U.S.

1930s

This effigy of a lynched black man was hung from a pole in Miami on May 3, 1939, as a warning to local African Americans to refrain from voting in elections. Lynching was employed across the South to enforce racial segregation from the 1860s through the 1930s. Attempts to pass federal anti-lynching laws were suppressed in the U.S. Senate for decades by a powerful Southern lobby.

1963

The movement for black civil rights, sparked by the U.S. Supreme Court's 1954 school desegregation decision and the successful 1955-56 boycott of the bus system in Montgomery, Ala., heated up in the 1960s as activists challenged segregation in the South. The Klan responded: on Sept. 15, 1963, members of a Klan offshoot group in Birmingham, Ala.,

set off a bomb in the 16th Street Baptist Church, a black congregation. Four girls, ages 11 to 14, were killed; 22 more people were injured. Klansman Robert Chambliss was convicted of the four murders in 1977; two other Klansmen were convicted in 2001-02, after the FBI and local prosecutors reopened the case. A fourth suspect, never charged, died in 1994. Above, a funeral service.

1960s

Klan members grew bolder throughout the 1960s, and the hoods that once ensured anonymity now rose above the faces, revealing identities. Above, Klan members, including women, bow their heads in prayer at a gathering in North Carolina, as captured by noted LIFE magazine photographer Charles Moore. From its beginnings, the Klan has often cloaked its agenda of racial division and its tactics of terrorism in the guise of devotion to patriotism, family values and Christian godliness.

2006

New members of the National Knights of the Ku Klux Klan savor their first cross-burning outside the town of Red Bay in Franklin County, Ala. Spurred by an economic slump and increasing racial diversity in the U.S., membership in white hate groups has risen sharply in recent years.

Stars, stripes and hoods *In the largest public display of Klan power in U.S. history, some 40,000 Klansmen participated in a march in Washington on Aug. 8, 1925.*

Above, Klan members drape the steps of the U.S. Capitol Building with a giant flag

continued to murder blacks and "immoral" whites, chiefly in the South.

During World War II, the Klan slept again. But in the 1950s and '60s the winds of black freedom awakened old fears, and rising once more to fight the civil rights movement, the Klan now operated as a loosely linked web of local hate groups rather than as a monolithic national organization. The crimes of the civil rights era in which Klan members played a role include the 1963 bombing of an Alabama church that killed four young black girls; the 1963 murder of civil rights pioneer Medgar Evers; the 1964 mutilation and murder of three civil rights workers in Mississippi; and many more. In many of these cases, justice was denied for decades: a number of long-time Klan members have been convicted of '60s-era crimes between 1990 and 2010.

While homegrown terrorists stalked the U.S. in the 1990s, such groups often took the form of anti-government militias, and the Klan stayed out of the headlines. But the presidential candidacy and election of Barack Obama, son of a white American mother and a Kenyan father, reignited the old flames

of white grievance. A grisly murder that took place in Bogalusa, La., in November 2008, illuminates the mind-set and makeup of today's Klan.

The story begins in the fall of 2008, when Cynthia Lynch, 43, scoured the Internet. Lean and almost 6 ft. tall, with hair cut nearly to her skull, Lynch lived alone in Tulsa, Okla., sustained by Social Security benefits granted early due to a mental illness. She landed on the website of the Sons of Dixie, a group that had been founded by Raymond (Chuck) Foster.

Foster, 44, was well known to authorities in St. Tammany Parish, north of New Orleans, and in neighboring Washington Parish, where he lived in the working-class town of Bogalusa (pop. roughly 13,000). Earlier this decade, he pleaded guilty to monetary instrument abuse charges—essentially forgery and selling counterfeit money. In 2001, he became founding Imperial Wizard of the Southern White Knights of the Ku Klux Klan. It launched chapters in Florida, Georgia and Ohio. Then, in 2005, it disbanded.

His next act was the Sons of Dixie, and he drew a cast of mostly twentysomething disciples. They set up a website to attract new recruits.

Enter Lynch, who took a bus from Tulsa to Slidell, La., in St. Tammany Parish. She apparently told relatives she was going to join a church. According to Sons of Dixie papers seized by Louisiana law enforcement authorities, Lynch was assessed on categories such as "Honesty," "Klannish Practices" and "Ambishous." Lynch's criminal record—she had been convicted of possessing methamphetamine in 2005—was so appealing to Foster, authorities say, that he waived the Sons of Dixie's $25 application fee.

Lynch arrived in Slidell on Friday, Nov. 7., three days after Obama's election. She was brought to Foster's rented, ranch-style compound in Bogalusa. Jack Strain Jr., the sheriff of St. Tammany Parish, told TIME that the initiation ceremony began swiftly and included the shaving of Lynch's head, the white hooded suits, the pledging of loyalty to the Klan, the burning of torches. It extended into Saturday. Then, on Sunday, Strain says, Foster led his group of disciples to an isolated campsite in the town of Sun (pop. barely 500) in St. Tammany Parish. About 5 p.m., Lynch apparently asked Foster to take her back to town, so she could return to Tulsa. She was reportedly homesick. Foster reportedly refused. She asked again. But, Strain says, Foster pushed her to the ground. She reportedly got up, and approached him. Just then, Strain says, Foster drew a gun, raised it to her chin and pulled the trigger.

"To give you a glimpse into the shooter's mindset," Strain told TIME, "after he shoots the young lady, he rolls her over, pulls the pocketknife out, and begins opening her back to extract the round … to destroy the evidence. Right where she fell." According to Strain, Foster then ordered his disciples to destroy the evidence. Two of them allegedly walked into a nearby convenience store and asked a clerk: How do you remove blood from clothing? The clerk called the authorities, and Lynch's body was soon found. Foster was arrested on a second-degree murder charge, while seven other disciples, including his son Shane, then 20, were arrested on obstruction of justice charges. As of early 2010, their trials had not yet begun. And America's trials with the Ku Klux Klan also seemed to be far from over. ∎

The Klan Today

The election of Barack Obama as America's first black President seemed to incite a violent revulsion among a few whites already dismayed by the economic crisis and swelling immigration. White supremacist groups and Internet forums like *Stormfront.org* reported a surge in interest. "I think there's a perfect storm coming together," Mark Potok, editor of the Southern Poverty Law Center's *Intelligence Report,* which tracks U.S. hate crimes, told TIME early in 2009.

Lance Hill, executive director of the Southern Institute for Education and Research at Tulane University, in New Orleans, has studied hate group activity for years. He was struck not only by the groups' resurgence but also by its members' youth and apparent embrace of hooded robes—symbols that in recent years had become passé for many white racists. Particularly given the presidential election's outcome, Hill says, "in the rural white South, there's a sense that they've become marginalized and are politically irrelevant to national politics. Taking up those robes and rituals of the Klan can be seen as an act of defiance," he says, adding, "That's a dangerous turn, because that kind of hopelessness can lead to more extremist and violent acts of desperation."

Joe Culpepper, captain of the Bogalusa, La., police force, told TIME that the Klan-related killing of newcomer Cynthia Lynch late in 2008 *(see main article)* "took us by surprise. We have our share of white trash up here. But the community has evolved past Klan-type behavior. Nobody is on that page anymore." His view was echoed by Andre Johnson, one of two blacks on the seven-member governing board of Washington Parish, who declared, "Although we have a history of racial divisiveness, it was an isolated incident. But as a whole, as a parish … we're trying to move toward the future." Also thinking of the future: the young couple below, who were married in a Klan-blessed ceremony elsewhere in Louisiana in 2008.

Conflicts of Blood and Oath

Italian and U.S. authorities are still battling history's most notorious secret crime society, the Mafia

The scene is familiar to millions if only through staged dramatizations on film or TV: in a darkened room, flanked by the secret society's local boss and his lieutenants, the initiate and his sponsor stand in front of a table on which are placed a gun and, on occasion, a knife. The boss picks up the gun and intones in the Sicilian dialect: *"Niatri representam La Cosa Nostra. Sta famigghiaè La Cosa Nostra* [We represent La Cosa Nostra. This family is Our Thing]." The sponsor then pricks his trigger finger and the trigger finger of the new member, holding both together to symbolize the mixing of blood. After swearing to hold the family above his religion, his country and his wife and children, the inductee finishes the ritual. A picture of a saint or a religious card is placed in his cupped hands and ignited. As the paper burns, the inductee, together with his sponsor, proclaims, "If I ever violate this oath, may I burn as this paper."

Through this rite, which adapts elements of Masonic ritual, young men are sworn into the most famous of secret criminal societies, the Mafia, or La Cosa Nostra, becoming "made men" or "wiseguys." They are joining an organization that today numbers perhaps only a few hundred thousand active members on a planet with 6.8 billion people—yet which exerts a magnetic fascination out of proportion to its actual size. Its activities run the gamut of criminality, from prostitution to loan-sharking to drug-trafficking to extortion to gambling. Yet despite the sordid nature of its activities, the Mafia bears an undeniable sheen of glamour—not least because it has been romanticized over recent decades in films, on TV and in popular novels. As Chicago-based Mafia-fighter Stephen Schiller told TIME in 1977, "We have made these bums folk heroes."

Yet the romance is based on something very real. Much of the public's fascination with Mafia life rests upon the complex moral code that undergirds it: these men who traffic in sleaze and human misery have convinced themselves that their commitment to La Cosa Nostra [Our Thing] supersedes all other values. In the Mafia code, an honorable man is the man who practices omertà, the code of silence; who pursues vendetta, the code of revenge; and who, per his initiation oath, values his loyalty to his fellow members of a criminal family above all others, including his personal family: his

Showing respect
Sicilian men kiss in 1978, right. Such old-world signs of deference are often associated with mob membership.

Above, a poster in Sicily seeks information on Mafia leader Bernardo Provenzano, who stayed in hiding for 43 years before he was captured in 2006

oath trumps his blood. The penalty for breaching these codes: death. In the tension between these conflicting values, the drama of Mob life is born.

The Sicilian Mafia is not the only organized crime gang to have flourished in Italy: Naples is home to the Camorra; Calabria has its 'Ndrangheta; Puglia is the home of the Sacra Corona Unita, or United Sacred Crown. But it is the Mafia whose tentacles reach deepest into its home soil, and which has transplanted itself most effectively around the world, including the U.S. While the modern Mafia's roots are traced to a protection racket that began operating in the Sicilian capital of Palermo in the 1860s, the code of the mafiosi has been shaped over the course of some 3,000 years, as Sicilians became clannish and insular as they fought wave after wave of hostile invaders. Sicilian men formed underground families that acted as vigilante groups against the outsiders, and those who served in these private societies were regarded as men of honor. Over time, the secret vigilante groups turned from protecting the innocent to offering protection, ensuring that those who didn't ante up paid a steep price in vandalism or a beating.

The Sicilian Mafia may have long fascinated the world with its mix of murder, mystery, codes of honor and Old World folklore. But according to TIME correspondent Jeff Israely, who has reported on the Mafia's activities for years from Italy, "the Mob is best understood as an organization constantly trying to consolidate its power in order to accumulate wealth." Considered the modern inventor of organized crime, the Sicilian Mob remains hugely powerful—but for the moment it is on the run, set back on its heels in an ongoing battle with authorities desperate to crush its influence. While it is far too early to declare victory, Italian police, prosecutors and judges have scored major successes in recent years.

The new round of warfare dates back to 1984, when on Sept. 29, authorities mounted a series of surprise raids on Mafia members, arresting more than 53 gangsters. The sweeping strategy hit La Cosa Nostra in the trenches, marking a critical victory for such crusading

Organized Crime in the U.S.
A rogues' gallery of racketeers, then and now

AL CAPONE
Taking control of the Chicago Mob in the 1920s, Capone and his "Syndicate," or "Outfit" presided over one of the most lawless of American eras, as Prohibition created a huge market for illegal liquor. Unable to rein in his vast and highly profitable empire of bootlegging, gambling and prostitution, federal authorities convicted him of tax evasion in 1931.

MEYER LANSKY
Lansky rose high in organized crime, though as a Jew he was not a sworn member of a Mafia family. He helped the Mob take control of Havana nightclubs and Las Vegas casinos, reaping rich rewards. But biographer Robert Lacey argues that Lansky, while a shrewd casino operator, was never the brilliant Mob mastermind he is cracked up to be.

LUCKY LUCIANO
The Sicilian-born Luciano reshaped the Mob, helping set up the five families of New York City (he was the first don of the Genovese family) and forming a national commission to preside over larger Mafia issues. TIME named him one of the 100 most important persons of the 20th century. Convicted in 1936, he was paroled in 1946 on condition that he return to Italy.

JOHN J. GOTTI
The poster boy for the modern Mob ran New York City's Gambino crime family after he ordered the 1985 murder of predecessor Paul Castellano. Gotti was known as the "Dapper Don" for his $1,800 suits and carefully coiffed hair. He was also called the "Teflon Don," eluding conviction for years. He was finally convicted in 1992 and died in prison 10 years later.

JOHN A. "JUNIOR" GOTTI
The son of the "Teflon Don" is believed to have helped his father run the Gambino family while the senior Gotti was in jail, and he has proved as slick as his father at avoiding conviction. In the years from 2004 through 2009, he was tried four times and never convicted. On Dec. 1, 2009, his latest trial ended in a hung jury, above, and federal prosecutors say they will not try him again.

Nabbed at last
Apprehended after eluding authorities since 1963, Mafia boss Bernardo Provenzano is taken into custody in April 2006.

Note that police are wearing hoods to ensure anonymity—essential in a society where vendetta, the code of revenge, sends the police into hiding, fugitives not from justice but from misplaced codes of honor

magistrates as Giovanni Falcone and Paolo Borsellino, who were lionized in the press for their courageous stand against the Mob.

In what became known as the Maxi-Trials that followed, Sicilian prosecutors tried hundreds of Mafia suspects en masse for crimes ranging from murder to criminal association. The trials, held in Palermo, made for great theater. Crammed together into a custom-made, bunker-like courtroom, the accused seemed straight from a Hollywood casting call for Mob thugs: often unshaven, sweaty and in short-sleeved leisure shirts, the Mafia men pointed fingers and hollered threats from inside steel cages that ringed the back of the vast, underground trial chamber.

Though prosecutors won more than 300 convictions by 1987, both Falcone and Borsellino paid the ultimate price for their Maxi-Trial assault. Falcone was killed, along with his wife and three bodyguards, when a bomb exploded in his car in Rome on May 23, 1992. Two months later, Borsellino and five bodyguards were killed outside the apartment of Borsellino's mother in Palermo, when a car packed with explosives was detonated by remote control. According to the U.S. FBI, Sicilian mafiosi have a special term for such high-ranking authorities, after they are assassinated: "excellent cadavers."

Rocked by the multiple homicides, Italian police cracked down: in 1993 Mafia boss Salvatore (Toto) Riina was arrested and subsequently sentenced for masterminding the Falcone and Borsellino assassinations. His place was taken by his childhood friend, Bernardo Provenzano, who had managed to elude authorities by remaining in hiding since 1963. He avoided capture for 13 more years after taking over, but in 2006, the capo, age 73, was finally arrested on the outskirts of his hometown of Corleone, a longtime bastion of the Sicilian Mob whose name was appropriated by American writer Mario Puzo for his fictional godfather, Don Corleone. Authorities say Provenzano, nicknamed "The Tractor" for his skills at mowing down rivals in his youth, had largely transformed La Cosa Nostra in his years as its capo into a less violent, more efficient economic machine.

A mere 18 months after Provenzano's capture, Italian authorities apprehended his successor, Salvatore Lo Piccolo, 65, along with his son Sandro, 32, whom he'd been grooming for succession. The Mob was clearly reeling. And the authorities scored another success in February 2008 when a joint FBI–Italian police action dubbed the "Old Bridge" netted 58 mobsters in and around New York City and 19 in and around Palermo. The operation focused on members of the Inzerillo Mob family of Palermo, who had been allowed under a Mob agreement to flee Sicily in the early 1980s, after Riina had decimated their ranks in a brutal internecine feud. The authorities nabbed the gang members, even as many of them were preparing to return to Sicily for the first time.

Ten months later, Italian authorities dealt yet another blow to the upper echelon of Sicily's legendary crime syndicate. On Dec. 16, 2008, in a sweeping police raid that stretched from Palermo to Tuscany and involved more than 1,200 carabinieri officers, 94 mafiosi were arrested. The action was directed at members of La Cupola, a kind of consultative board of regional bosses, who met from time to time to resolve internal disputes and forge long-term strategy.

Italian investigators said those taken into custody had been attempting to re-establish the authority of La Cupola to solidify the Mafia's power structure after a leadership vacuum had followed the earlier, high-profile arrests of Provenzano and Lo Piccolo. Leading anti-Mob magistrate Pietro Grasso boasted that police operations over the past few years had put La Cosa Nostra on its knees.

The new roundup, he declared, "keeps it from getting up."

Yet the road to a Mafia-free Sicily will not be easy; authorities are fighting a culture that has grown up over some 3,000 years. Back in 1984, when the current crusade against the Mob began in Sicily, a businessman in Palermo told TIME, "Our city administration is so bad that without the 'friends of friends,' how are we ever going to get anything accomplished? At least with the Mafia, you knew how to fiddle it." His comment rings just as true a quarter-century later.

It was also in 1984 that Pope John Paul II traveled to Sicily and called upon listeners to break "the tragic chain of vendettas" and abandon the Mob's code of silence, "which binds so many people in a type of squalid complicity dictated by fear." Inspiring words, but they fell on deaf ears. In 2008, New York State Attorney General Andrew Cuomo, who helped lead the "Old Bridge" sting, declared, "Organized crime still exists. We like to think it's a vestige of the past. It's not. It is as unrelenting as weeds that continue to sprout in the cracks in society." Those cracks are simply the fault lines of individual failings writ large, and barring a seismic shift in human nature, it is hard to imagine a world without the Mafia. ■

Never again
Citizens have gathered in Palermo, Sicily, and in other Italian cities, to march against organized crime every year since the murder of two crusading magistrates by the Mafia rocked the nation in 1992. At right, the first march in Palermo

The Mob on The Screen

Hollywood's first films about organized crime were shoot-'em-up westerns transplanted to the city. But with his first two *Godfather* films, Francis Ford Coppola showed that Mafia life could be a source for rich, dark drama. They became as much a touchstone within the Mob as without. Rudolph Giuliani, a former Mafia-busting prosecutor, said that after the films were released, real-life gangsters starting speaking like the characters in them.

Little Caesar

Mervyn LeRoy's 1931 Warner Bros. film starring Edward J. Robinson as Caesar Enrico Bandello, a.k.a. "Rico," was a huge hit that exploited gangster life for its sensational aspects but denatured the Mob of its Italian roots. Robinson's portrayal of an Al Capone–style gangster was so compelling that it locked him into playing Mafia tough guys for the rest of his career—a surprising turn of events for a man born Emanuel Goldenberg to Yiddish-speaking Jewish parents in Bucharest, Romania.

The *Godfather* Trilogy

Francis Ford Coppola's brilliant films about Mafia life in the U.S. are true tragedies, documenting how loyalty to the larger crime family can erode all human ties to one's own family. But they also represent a sort of love letter to the Mafia, gilding the Mob in a rich patina of sentiment. As TIME's James Poniewozik argued, "*The Godfather I* and *II* were nostalgia movies, harking back to the glory years of a racket whose best years were behind it even in the '70s. They held up myths of honor among thieves—we don't sell drugs, we don't kill civilians ... that [were later abandoned], if they ever existed."

GoodFellas

Martin Scorsese's 1990 film showed Mafia life's glamour, as in a gangster's stunning entrance into the Copacabana nightclub. It also got closer to the stupidity and venality of Mob life, said TIME's Poniewozik. Even so, wiseguys embraced the film: it told them that they were still somebodies, not nobodies.

The Sopranos

Writer David Chase's much-admired HBO series yanked the Mob into the present day with its portrait of a don, Tony Soprano (played by a solid James Gandolfini), so conflicted he enters psychoanalysis.

Showing the Colors

From Colombia to Japan to New York City, the signs and symbols of criminal gangs may vary, but the values of their members are remarkably similar: allegiance to the Mob is the highest virtue

Digital information

Above, Bloods in Corona, a Queens, N.Y. neighborhood, display the "five-point star" gang sign in 2007.

At left, members of a Bloods gang, or "set," attend a funeral for a young man slain by police in 2006 in Jamaica, a nearby area in Queens

U.S. Street Gangs

The two best-known U.S. criminal street gangs are the Crips and Bloods, and their rivalry compares with that of the Capulets and Montagues—and is often, sadly, just as romanticized. The Crips, Bloods, Latin Kings and other street gangs may have a certain style, but they represent little more than a colorful dead end for the teenagers they attract. And though the Crips and Bloods remain the two largest and most notorious of America's street gangs, they are not necessarily representative of today's evolving gangs. According to the FBI, which is charged with monitoring such groups on a national level, gangs are migrating from urban areas to suburban and rural communities—which are showing an uptick in crime as a result.

As of 2010, the federal agency believes that some 20,000 violent street gangs, motorcycle gangs and prison gangs with approximately 1 million members are criminally active in the U.S. Gang members com-

mit as much as 80% of the crime in many communities, according to law enforcement officials, and they are the primary retail-level distributors of most illicit drugs used in the U.S. One fact that hasn't changed over the years: as Los Angeles County District Attorney Ira Reiner told Time in the wake of the 1992 Rodney King riots, which devastated the city's poorer neighborhoods: "Each one [gang member] is a mini crime wave, and together they are a major crime wave."

Unlike the Mafia or the Ku Klux Klan, U.S. street gangs, like Japan's yakuza, are among the crime-friendly societies whose members make no secret of their affiliation; on the contrary, membership has its privileges, and the chance to wear gang colors and throw gang signs are among the coveted rewards of admission to the club. For the record: the Crips' colors are blue, the Bloods' colors are red. There is no purple in the gangsters' palette.

The Yakuza

To most Japanese, the yakuza are as instantly recognizable as soldiers in an enemy army. They wear their hair in crewcuts, parade about in flashy double-breasted suits and adopt the tough-guy scowl of characters out of *Guys and Dolls*. Beneath those suits, many sport full-body tattoos, *irezumi*, that are created by hand rather than electric needles. A member who violates the gang's code may express remorse by slicing off the tip of his little finger and handing it to his superior.

The yakuza (bad-hands) are part of a Japanese chivalric tradition that dates back to the 17th century, when unemployed samurai turned to banditry. Their star has faded of late: thanks to an anti-gang law directed at them in 1992, membership has dropped to some 87,000—though the yakuza still constitute one of the world's largest organized crime syndicates.

The Death of Pablo Escobar, Fernando Botero, 1999

Narcotraficantes

By TIME's estimate, when Colombian crime boss Pablo Escobar was gunned down on a rooftop on Medellín in 1993, below, the drug-related violence led by his gang of *narcotraficantes* had cost Colombia the lives of an attorney general, a Justice Minister, three presidential candidates, more than 200 judges, 30 kidnap victims, dozens of journalists and some 1,000 police officers in the previous 10 years.

Along the way, Escobar had lived large, famously hiding out in a remote jungle enclave that included a personal menagerie. Even today, many young Colombians still view Escobar as the romantic, larger-than-life figure depicted by Ferdinand Botero in the 1999 painting above and remain tempted by the wealth and power of a new generation of drug lords.

One such figure is Mexico's top drug chieftain Joaquín Guzmán: the most wanted man in his nation has eluded capture for years. Two places he can be found: at No. 701 on the *Forbes* magazine list of the world's richest people—and on TIME's list of the 100 Most Influential People of 2009.

Key to Photographs, Introduction

Pyramid and All-Seeing Eye, reverse of U.S. $1 bill

Glass pyramid, Courtyard of the Louvre Museum, Paris. Architect: I.M. Pei

The Magic Flute, *set design, Metropolitan Opera, New York City. Designer: Julie Taymor*

The Ancient of Days, *watercolor with relief etching. Artist: William Blake*

Stamp with symbols of Freemasonry (reversed for readability)

George Washington Masonic Memorial, Alexandria, Va. Architects: Helmle & Corbett

Statue of George Washington, U.S. Capitol Rotunda, Washington, D.C.

Dome, St. Peter's Basilica, Rome. Architect: Donato Bramante

Main Reading Room, Library of Congress (Jefferson Building), Washington, D.C.

Fountain of the Four Rivers, Rome. Architect: Gianlorenzo Bernini

Washington Monument, Washington, D.C. Architect: Robert Mills

Gnomon, Church of St. Sulpice, Paris